TALKING AT TRENA'S

Everyday Conversations at an African American Tavern

Reuben A. Buford May

NEW YORK UNIVERSITY PRESS

New York and London

New York University Press
New York and London

© 2001 by New York University

Library of Congress Cataloging-in-Publication Data
May, Reuben A. Buford, 1965–
Talking at Trena's : everyday conversations at an African American
tavern / Reuben A. Buford May.
p. cm.
Includes bibliographical references and index.
ISBN 0-8147-5671-9 (acid-free paper) —
ISBN 0-8147-5672-7 (pbk. : acid-free paper)
1. African Americans—Race identity. 2. African Americans—
Attitudes. 3. African Americans—Social life and customs. 4. Middle class—
United States—Attitudes. 5. Middle class—United States—Social life and
customs. 6. Social interaction—United States—Case studies. 7. United
States—Race relations—Case studies. 8. Racism—United States—
Psychological aspects—Case studies. 9. Bars (Drinking establishments)—
Illinois—Chicago. 10. Chicago (Ill.)—Race relations. I. Title.
E185.625 .M35 2001
305.896073—dc21   2001001495

Manufactured in the United States of America
10 9 8 7 6 5 4 3 2 1

*This book is dedicated to the memory of my grandfather
Nelson Rushing, my father, Bill Cody, and
my uncle Mickey Holmes.*

CONTENTS

ACKNOWLEDGMENTS

From the summer of 1994 to the winter of 1996, I did fieldwork in a neighborhood tavern I call Trena's. I had originally begun my research in neighborhood taverns as part of a larger comparative study of race and social organization. This comparative study, under the direction of William Julius Wilson and Richard P. Taub at the University of Chicago, examined the lifestyles, attitudes, and behaviors of residents in four racially and ethnically distinct neighborhoods in order to determine the extent to which each of the neighborhoods' residents achieved the communal goals of social organization. What grew out of my participation in this larger study was an interest in how patrons in racially segregated neighborhood taverns talked specifically about race and contemporary issues generated by television. I wanted to get some sense of how African Americans, within the context of a "safe" haven, made sense of their lives in a society that emphasizes race and racial identity. As an African American myself, I found this question of not only sociological but also personal interest.

This book is an ethnographic study of middle-class African Americans in the relaxed setting of a neighborhood tavern. I explore the underlying themes related to the everyday lives of Trena's patrons. By immersing myself in the daily routines of leisure at Trena's, I learned how patrons' talk conveyed the subtle ways in which issues of race penetrated everyday life. Talking, drinking, and laughing with the patrons while using a sociological eye gave me an opportunity to look more deeply into the taken-for-granted processes by which so many African Americans understand race.

There are many who deserve thanks for supporting me during my young professional career. William Julius Wilson provided guidance and an environment—the Center for the Study of Inequality at the University of Chicago—for my intellectual growth. Richard P. Taub, Edgar Epps, and Kenneth Watson provided invaluable direction, while allowing me to grow as an individual scholar. Many of the ideas developed in this book were reformulated on the basis of hours of informal dialogue with my colleagues and friends Alford Young, Jolyon Wurr, Mary Pattillo-McCoy, Sandra Smith, Mignon Moore, Pamela Cook, Sarita Gregory, Ray Reagans, Fred Hutchinson, Carla O'Connor, and Peter Schneeburger. My skills as an ethnographer were developed and refined through discussions with Erin Augis, Patrick Carr, Monica Escurra, Chenoa Flippen, Jennifer Johnson, Maria Kefalas, Jennifer Pashup-Graham, and Monica Ibanez.

Others who provided moral and intellectual support along the way include Andrew Abbott, Linda Waite, Jeanine Hildreth, George Wimberly III, Lori Hill, Julian Go, Nick Young, Ezra Zuckerman, Jeffery Morenoff, and Sharon Hicks-Bartlett. When

I needed a break from the rigors of writing or help working through some of my ideas, I turned to my cybergroup "think tank" of friends. I owe Ray, Pegs, Mary, Ma P, Sheri, Nikki, Ada, Shelby "da playa," and Michael many thanks for helping me work out the kinks. My colleagues at the University of Georgia, especially Woody Beck, Linda Grant, Jim Dowd, Barry Schwartz, Michael Hodge, and Gary Alan Fine (now at Northwestern), also provided feedback and encouragement. I also owe thanks to the University of Georgia women's basketball team and head coach Andy Landers, and the Clarke Central High School boys basketball team and head coach Billy Wade. They helped me maintain a social life away from my work.

I believe that family support is most important when one sets out to achieve goals. This is probably because I have a supportive family. First, I thank my wife, Lyndel, who provided moral support throughout my graduate studies and subsequent research. I also thank my stepdaughter, Tamarra, and my daughter, "Big Ol" Gina May, for the simple distractions from sociology that they provided. I owe other members of my family thanks for their continued support, especially my mother, Gwendolyn May-Barlow, my stepfather, Michael Barlow, my youngest brother, Khary, and my "middlebruh," Tim. My best friend, Vic, provided me a life away from research and Bob Thurman provided me with "solutions" to many everyday problems. I love you all.

Chapters 3 and 4 are based on journal articles previously published. For permission to include this material I would like to thank the following: Sage Periodical Press, for permission to use "Tavern Culture and Television Viewing: The Influence of Local Viewing Culture on Patrons' Reception of Television Programs," *Journal of Contemporary Ethnography* 21(1) (1999) pp. 69–99, which appears in revised and expanded form in chapter 3; and Human Sciences Press, for permission to use "Race Talk and

Local Collective Memory among African American Men in a Neighborhood Tavern," *Qualitative Sociology* 23(2) (2000) pp. 201–214, which appears in revised and expanded form as part of chapter 4.

Finally, this study could not have been completed without the help of the patrons in Trena's. I would like to thank them for willingly sharing with me intimate details about their personal lives. While I cannot thank them individually, I must recognize their contributions to my personal knowledge and my sociological knowledge. It is my hope that, by understanding their lives, we can better understand our own.

INTRODUCTION

As a young boy, I loved to go over to my grandfather's house on Saturday morning, when he used to cut hair in his living room. It was not so much that I wanted to watch him work as it was to listen as the regular customers, Duke, Hank, Phil, and the others, told stories and talked to one another and the television. Often I was so drawn to the intimate exchanges among these men that my grandmother had to chase me outside to play with my peers. In the African American community, barber shops, like the one my grandfather once owned, have long served as one of the places where people who live in the same neighborhood and share many values can gather to discuss their common social problems and enjoy the diversity of the African American life experience. The neighborhood tavern is another such haven.

Years later, when I was a graduate student, I decided to explore face-to-face social interaction among African Americans in a semipublic setting that included television as a source of conversation. I thought that understanding African Americans' varied life experiences—talked about within the context of a racially homogeneous setting—was one key to understanding the complex nature of racial attitudes. Thus, I began my study of Trena's,[1] an African American neighborhood tavern.

This book is an account of my experiences at Trena's. It reveals how middle-class African Americans make sense of life's complexities by using a neighborhood tavern as a safe haven to freely share their feelings about race, sex, television, and work. It recognizes tavern talk not just as the byproduct of social play and symbolic performance in the tavern but also as an indication of the social problems African Americans confront daily. It exposes middle-class African Americans' feelings of vulnerability, especially in light of events such as racially motivated attacks against Blacks and challenges to social programs, like affirmative action, that have been responsible for the expansion of the Black middle class.

This ethnographic study follows a long tradition of scholarly research on the significance of social interaction in informal gathering places like the neighborhood tavern. Ethnographies written in the late 1960s and early 1970s, such as those by Sherri Cavan and E. E. LeMasters, have confirmed the importance of neighborhood drinking establishments as gathering places where patrons go to escape the pressure of everyday life and to participate in a world of fun and play.[2] The work of Elijah Anderson took a closer look at social interaction in a neighborhood bar by documenting African American males' use of a complex stratification system to show deference to one another within the bar.[3] Building on the notion of the neighborhood tavern as a place for play, Michael Bell's work from the early 1980s also examined African Americans' social interaction.[4] Bell was particularly concerned with middle-class African Americans' creative self-expression within the context of the tavern.

More recently, Ray Oldenburg's research from the late 1980s and early 1990s reiterated the importance of informal gathering places as settings of leisure.[5] Oldenburg suggested that taverns, bars, and coffee houses continue to be places of escape as societies become more technologically advanced. While these works focus mostly on the social significance of the tavern for fun and play, they give little attention to how patrons' social lives within the tavern are influenced by their daily experiences outside the tavern.

In this book, I take a different approach. I uncover how patrons use tavern talk to make sense of their everyday experiences from the world beyond the tavern. More specifically, I reveal, through description and analysis of ethnographic data, how African Americans come to understand the underlying racial themes that exist on their jobs, in the television programs they view, and in their relationships with others. I place the patrons' tavern experience squarely on the shoulders of their feelings regarding race—a central fact in their everyday lives—and demonstrate how African Americans transform an informal social world of fun and play into a social world where they can learn strategies for defending their social status from the threat of economic and political forces beyond their control.

Trena's, like every other drinking establishment, has its own social characteristics that make it unique. Still, many of its social characteristics are common to a variety of informal gathering places and the people that frequent them. These commonalities make studying social life in a tavern viable for understanding social relationships more broadly. In chapter 1 I describe social life within Trena's in order to provide information useful for understanding patrons' talk in Trena's and the broader arguments I make in subsequent chapters. I introduce the kinds of people that frequent the tavern, their normative expectations for interaction, and their use of video games, music, and television to draw others into conversation. Although I present a brief description of a group of patrons and refer to them throughout the book, I have given greater emphasis to their general characteristics than to their specific roles as characters in a chronological or sequential narrative. This slice of tavern life conveys the general nature of tavern talk and allows for a wider application of the sociological ideas presented.

Like Elijah Anderson's study of Jelly's, an African American drinking establishment in Chicago, the current book recognizes the social significance of patrons' employment status within the tavern. Anderson demonstrated the ways in which *Jelly's* patrons' social status in the tavern was linked to their broader employment status outside the tavern. Through his description of "the regulars," "the wineheads," and "the hoodlums," Anderson explained how employment or unemployment pressures bear down on the men of Jelly's, who in turn develop rules for deference based on such status.[6] Unlike Anderson's observations, however, the current study links employment status to tavern social life in a less stratified way. The patrons' individual work experience, grounded in opportunity created by civil rights legislation and an expanding economy, provides a source of individual legitimacy, as well as concrete and abstract resources for the patrons as a whole. In chapter 2, I explore the relationship between patrons' employment status and the social life of the tavern. I describe patrons' employment experiences, their perception of life chances related to work, and their incorporation of themes from work into conversation. I conclude this chapter with a discussion of how patrons view employment prospects for African Americans as a racial group.

Work experience is one basis for conversation among the patrons within the tavern, another is what the patrons view on television. The prominence of television viewing in America has had profound effects on the way many Americans think about the world around them. Some social critics, troubled by what they view as the deterioration of American values, have been concerned with the impact that television programming has on its viewers. Given the influence that television has on how Americans view the world, I examine ways that patrons construct the meaning of television while viewing it within Trena's. In chapter 3, I demonstrate how patrons interpret television themes through their own personal experiences, develop imaginary one-sided relationships with television characters, evaluate mass media information, and create racial frames through which they view Whites' behavior. I specify how patrons' transformation of typical media information becomes a socially meaningful experience that helps patrons shape their own racial identity.

Trena's patrons affirm their African American identity through race talk—conversation that focuses on some aspect of being African American. In chapter 4, I explore race talk within the tavern by examining patrons' narratives of racial conflict, their perceptions of racism and discrimination, and their individual and racial group self-criticism. I suggest that patrons' retelling of negative racial experiences has a compounding effect that is felt by others beyond the participants in the original encounter. This effect is the legacy of negative racial encounters and continues to have residual influence on African Americans' beliefs and attitudes regarding interracial interaction.

In addition to focusing on race as a central theme of discussion, patrons also discuss male-female relationships. Through their talk, patrons suggest explanations for the high number of divorces and separations among African American couples.[7] In chapter 5, I demonstrate how patrons make sense of marital issues, come to terms with divorce and separation, and negotiate the tavern as a "man's place." I conclude with a discussion of how traditional tavern culture influences patrons' outlook on male-female relationships.

Like so many other informal settings, Trena's is a place where patrons not only consider serious social issues but engage in verbal games of sex talk. In chapter 6, I look at episodes of sex talk as a form of play, as the bartender's dramatic performance, and as the patrons' exercise of symbolic power. I conclude with a discussion of how sex talk maintains traditional notions of masculinity that focus on heterosexuality and male dominance in male-female relationships.

In chapter 7, I take the observations made in the previous chapters and weave them into a theoretical statement about the significance of informal social settings like the tavern. I focus on the specific ways that participants in racially homogeneous settings develop their view of the world around them and how that outlook can affect, more broadly, interracial interaction. I discuss the paradox of social relations within racially homogeneous settings—the extent to which tavern talk allows patrons to share in cathartic relief from the pressures of interracial interaction, while at the same time fortifying patrons' negative racial experiences.

Finally, in the appendix, I discuss the methodological concerns that face those doing ethnography in the tavern. My role, the expectations that others had of me, and the ways in which my own background influenced how I viewed the patrons within the tavern are brought to the fore.

Since the tavern continues to be a place for the patrons to express their everyday concerns, I have found it appropriate to write mostly in the "ethnographic present," writing events as if they are occurring in the present.[8] Each time I have returned to

Chicago and visited Trena's, I have found the regulars and bartender engaged in their lively discussions.[9] It is in recognizing this regular occurrence, the centrality of race in the patrons' everyday lives and the continued prevalence of racism and discrimination, that I write about Trena's in the present.

Chapter One

TRENA'S: A STUDY IN TAVERN CULTURE

It don't matter what you drink in here. This tavern is not just a place to drink—what a person has in their glass is not as important as what they talk about.

Before I entered Trena's for the first time, I knew that it was one of several businesses and services located in South Gate, an African American, middle-class neighborhood, on the south side of Chicago. I had passed Trena's many times before while driving along Eighth Avenue, South Gate's main neighborhood thoroughfare. There were other businesses along Eighth Avenue, such as Phipp's dry cleaners, Stop-n-Go grocery, McDonald's, Amoco, and Johns Associates' dental office. Across the street, to the north of Trena's, were several well-kept single-family homes. These three-bedroom homes, built during the late 1940s, were once owned by Whites who surrendered the neighborhood during the influx of African Americans to South Gate in the 1960s and 1970s.[1] To the south of Trena's were more single-family homes and a mixture of two- and three-flat apartment buildings. What I did not know about Trena's, however, was that the Eighth Avenue door was usually locked during the daytime business hours and that the only way to enter was through the west door.

One afternoon, while driving down Eighth Avenue, I decided to check out Trena's. When I arrived at Trena's, I parked my car on the west side and walked around the building to what appeared to be the main entrance on Eighth Avenue. Dressed in shorts, a T-shirt, and a baseball cap, I approached the entrance and pulled the door. It was locked. I peered through the glass door and noticed several patrons enjoying drinks and conversation. They were ignoring my presence. I was sure the tavern was open, so I waited for someone to let me in. No one responded. Confused by the patrons' behavior, I walked around to the west side of the building. I pulled the door, and it opened. I was embarrassed. I had not known what the regulars knew. The bartenders always locked the front door during the day. This mistake set me apart as an outsider, hardly a position I wanted to be in while trying to gain access to Trena's semipublic setting.

As I walked into the blue-and-white-trimmed small brick tavern, I was immediately followed by a short older man who I later discovered was Thompson, a long-time regular. His presence, as a familiar face, and my entrance "with" him suggested to the other patrons that I must be okay. Once inside, I took a quick glance around the room to find the first available seat. All of the eight or so patrons seemed to stare at me when I entered, but, once I sat down, most of them continued their conversation, and I had a chance to look around. What first caught my attention was the two slot machine video games directly across from me. I had never seen games like those in my visits to other taverns. As I sat looking at the video games, large wall mirrors, and hanging pictures of Trena's staff, Lelia, one of the bartenders, approached from inside the triangular-shaped bar. She was tall, attractive, and dark skinned, and wore a white tuxedo shirt and a snug-fitting black skirt.

"How are you doing? I'm Lelia. What can I get for you this afternoon?" she said.

"I'm fine. I'll have an Amaretto Stone Sour," I replied. Lelia reached above her head to the glass rack that hung over the center of the bar and grabbed a glass. She walked around the other side of the island, where the liquor was stocked, to the blender and began mixing my drink. I sat quietly staring out of the large picture windows that faced Eighth Avenue until Lelia returned and set my drink on the bar.

"Here you go," she said.

"Thanks," I replied. She turned away and started for the other side of the bar near the CD jukebox. Someone had dropped a dollar in the jukebox and selected Bobby Brown's "My Prerogative," but no one seemed to be paying much attention to the juke box or to the two color televisions at opposite ends of the tavern. People were busy talking to one another. Still feeling embarrassed about my blundered entrance, I sat sipping my drink and glancing at the lavender-colored bar stools, the blue-gray carpeting, the pay phone, and the televisions. In the ten minutes I spent drinking, I made little eye contact with the other patrons, since they seemed guarded because of my presence. As I finished my drink, Lelia, with almost perfect timing, returned and flashed me a smile.

"Can I get you another one?" she asked in an encouraging voice.

"No, I'll just pay you now," I said. "How much do I owe you?"

"Four fifty."

"Here you go," I said, as I handed her a ten-dollar bill. She walked to the cash register near the open end of the bar, rang up the drink, and returned with my change. I took the money, separated two singles, and placed them on the bar under my empty glass.

"That's for you," I said.
"Thank you. You should come by again," she said flirtatiously.
"I will," I smiled and then I left the tavern.

Although Lelia was attractive, polite, and a skilled drink maker—all important characteristics for tending bar—she worked at Trena's for only a short time during my study. In my brief encounters with her, I would learn that she lacked the patience to deal with the informality of tavern relations, and it showed in her work. More important, she had "sticky fingers" and had been caught one evening stealing cash from the register at the end of her shift. She was one of three bartenders hired and fired for various reasons over the two-plus years I "hung out" at Trena's.

During my frequent visits to Trena's over the following couple of weeks, I maintained a low-key demeanor. On the day that I made my first foray into the active social life of the tavern, I found myself sitting a couple of stools away from two regulars, Tom and Steve. They were discussing how people should maintain respect for one another. I made eye contact with Tom as he spoke to Steve and nodded my head in agreement. Tom accepted my social overture, and as he continued talking to Steve he now included me in the conversation by making eye contact and increasing the volume of his voice. Later, when Steve moved to another conversation group, I eased over to the stool closest to Tom, and we continued to talk. Actually, I spent most of my time listening and offering affirmative "uh-huh"s and nods. When I finished my drink and was ready to leave, I shook Tom's hand and thanked him for the conversation. This marked the beginning of my move into the circle of the regulars.

As a thirty-year-old African American, I found that my presence in Trena's seemed to draw the older patrons to me. They wanted to share their experiences with a young man who could benefit from them. Even though I was able to engage in talk with several patrons, it was Monique, the regular bartender, who proved to be the most important facilitator of social engagement between me and the regulars. It took only a few visits before Monique knew me by what I drank. She would often ask, "Do you want the usual?" I had established my tavern identity as a listener, but I soon confronted the dilemma of presenting my dual role as a patron and a researcher. One day I decided to share my research objectives with Monique. When Monique returned with my drink, I said,

> "You know I'm in school right?"
>
> "Uh huh."
>
> "Well, yesterday I met with my professors, and they asked me what I was going to do since I gotta write this big paper to graduate. You know what I told them? I said, 'Fuck it. I'll write about hanging out in a tavern, Trena's.'"
>
> "Really," she said with a laugh.
>
> "Yeah. I'ma come up here and hang out with y'all for a year or so and write up a coupla notes and then write my paper and graduate and be Dr. May."
>
> "For real?"
>
> "Yeah."

After telling Monique about my research, I spent the next few weeks sharing this information with other patrons. If they did not know I was writing about the tavern for school, Monique was certain to tell them.

> As I sat sipping the last of my drink so that I could leave, Charles, a short, dark-skinned, fifty-year-old patron with whom I had talked previously, walked around the bar and said,
>
> "Let me come over here and talk to you before you get away."

I smiled at him and said, "How you doin'?"

"Fine," he replied as he walked around the back of my chair and had a seat at the bar. He lit a cigarette and asked, "How's the family?"

"Fine."

"What about the kids?"

"Fine. But I only have one kid."

"One kid? I thought you said your wife was pregnant. That's why I came over to see how things were going."

"Naw, she's not pregnant. We goin' do that some time this year, though."

Monique leaned over our end of the bar and said to me, "Why you goin' do that? This world is too cruel to children. They need things."

"That's why I'ma do it when I think that I am close to getting done with school. Then I can get a job."

"How long you got to go in school?" Charles asked.

"I'd say a year or so. I'm working on my Ph.D."

"Yeah, he's studying us," Monique said with a smile.

"Yeah, I'm studying what it's like to hang out in the bar. So I sit in here and listen to the stuff y'all say, and then I go home and write it up."

"So you working on your . . . thesis?" Charles asked.

"Yeah. That's exactly right," I said proudly.

"I just had a friend of mine get his doctorate," Charles said.

"What did he get it in?" I asked Charles.

"He got it in education. He's the principal of a school now."

Throughout my time at Trena's, my research seemed to be an innocent undertaking to the patrons. Those with whom I had long-standing contact were most aware of my research. Several regulars even took an interest, proposing a variety of research topics. Sometimes they would carry on a joke or tale and turn to me and say, "Yo, man. Make sure you get this shit in your book." After a few weeks, patrons' discussion of my research subsided, although several regulars stayed aware of my dual role. Monique especially remained cognizant of my patron-researcher role, just as she remained aware of the other regulars' various identities.

The Bartender: Monique

The bartender is an integral part of the social atmosphere in neighborhood taverns.[2] Monique is no exception. As the regular bartender during the afternoon and early evening hours, she creates Trena's social atmosphere. She carries her five-foot seven-inch frame with confidence. Her light brown skin, dark brown eyes, and full lips are accented by her dark brown freckles. Monique styles her long, wavy, black hair into a "ponytail" that whips back and forth as she moves around the bar. She wears her white tuxedo shirt and black pants fit snug.

Most of the men think that Monique is attractive. They flirt with her in games of sexual innuendo. On occasion Monique leads the discussion by bragging about how good she looks or how she can "wear 'em out." Some days Monique "turns the tables" on the regulars by flirting herself. She chooses a particular patron as her boyfriend for the day, and if another regular flirts with her she notifies her boyfriend, who comes to her aid. On other days, Monique plays the unwilling object of affection.

As we were sipping our drinks, Bobby said to Monique, "Boy, I wouldn't mind having sex with you." Monique replied, "I said no. Don't you understand?" Slick looked at Bobby and said, "I asked her about gettin' wit' her and she told me no, too. So I stopped.

*See, I understand English." Bobby responded, "Me no undastan'
no Englis' and no se habla español, either."*

*We laughed, and Monique shook her head from side to side
vigorously as she said to Bobby, "But you understand sign language. No, muthafucka."*

This game of sex talk is part of Monique's effort to make the
tavern a place of fun and play. If patrons enjoy themselves, they
will return to Trena's. They become an important source of income for Monique, who makes only thirty-five dollars a day
during her 10:00 A.M. to 6:00 P.M. shift.

Monique shows a great deal of frustration on slow business
days because fewer patrons mean fewer tips. She counts on her
tips to support her family of three. As a thirty-year-old single
parent, Monique acknowledges, "It's tough trying to take care of
a twelve-year-old daughter and a fourteen-year-old son when
you ain't making tips." Monique works hard to provide for her
children, who are a source of pride, especially her son, Colby,
who makes As and Bs in school. Her daughter, Carla, is often
jealous of her older brother and is much more difficult to deal
with. At one time, Monique was engaged to a correctional officer
trainee, but she broke off the engagement when he refused to
drive home seventy-five miles from Joliet, Illinois, to visit her
after his weekend training assignment. "That was just one of
many things that he did," she once remarked.

Inside the tavern, Monique joins the regulars in conversation,
using the full range of profanity expected in an informal setting
where people express themselves freely. She can be heard talking about "weird bitches," "crazy niggas," "silly muthafuckas,"
"dumb shits," "stupid fucks," and "damn hos" in a style and flavor consistent with traditional masculine tavern culture.[3] Not
only does Monique talk like a patron; from time to time she
"pours herself a little drink" or has a beer while she is working.

After she finished mixing my drink, she picked up a Malibu Rum bottle and poured some into a fancy glass with gold trim. I thought it was for a customer, but as she walked away she said in a lighthearted voice to the lady sitting across from me, "I had to fix me one. And don't y'all say shit 'cause y'all having one, too." Then Monique pretended to have a dialogue with the owner about drinking while she worked, "Well, you can't blame me, boss, 'cause they having one. It's they fault they all having one." We all laughed.

Monique's drinking is not limited to sips behind the bar but includes sitting next to patrons and drinking. By having a drink in this way, Monique transcends the traditional role of bartender. She becomes a social equal looking to have fun.

Monique poured herself some Bacardi and said to the two ladies across the bar, "Just a little bit."

"Oh, go 'head, girl. A little won't hurt," Louise said supportingly.

Monique walked from behind the bar and sat down on a stool, saying, "Shit, the way I feel, I'll fuck around and get drunk and tell y'all to mix yo' own damn drinks. Then tell ya to pay for whatcha drink. Just ring it up and put it in the cash register for yourself." We laughed.

Monique's behavior is like that of a patron with the added responsibility of making certain that others have things to drink and topics to talk about. Terrence and Trena, a married couple in their sixties and owners of the tavern, are rarely present during the daytime. They treat Monique as a manager and trust her with decisions made about the tavern. Monique's status with the owners gives her the opportunity to put her own special touch on Trena's. That touch includes making the bartender a full participant in the social activities within the tavern.

The Regulars

Just what type of patron goes to a drinking place like Trena's and hangs out and talks with friends all afternoon? After hanging at Trena's for a few weeks myself, I discovered a core group of regulars. Trena's regulars consist of a group of about thirty-five patrons, mostly men. They range in age from their late twenties to their early seventies, with the largest group in their early fifties. Most of the men are employed in a variety of skilled and unskilled occupations, and some are retired. Many of the working men have schedules that allow them to stop by Trena's for a drink on the way to or from work. No matter what time of day or afternoon, there is usually one or more of the regulars present at Trena's. Other than the all-female bartender staff, few women frequent Trena's during the regulars' time. They work in the neighborhood as office assistants and sales clerks and often come to the lounge on their lunch breaks. The men welcome these women because of their relationship with Monique, but to the men and women Trena's remains a "man's place," a place where men emphasize face-to-face interaction and assert traditional notions of masculinity.

Two identifiable groups of patrons use the tavern. One group uses Trena's during the noon and early evening hours and constitutes the "regular" stable clientele. They come to Trena's from the immediate neighborhood or other nearby African American communities. The other group, mostly anonymous patrons, use Trena's for late-evening, night, and weekend social activity. The "regular" group is the most interesting of the two because the patrons are engaged in frequent face-to-face interactions and are familiar with one another.

Although I present some of the individual patrons by name, my brief description of them is made in an effort to capture the characteristics of the average patron who frequents Trena's, rather than to fully describe individual characters who might appear in a chronological narrative of tavern life. Here are a few of those familiar faces at Trena's.

One of the first patrons who "schooled" me about life in and outside the tavern was James, a sixty-seven-year-old retired manufacturing worker who moved to Chicago from South Carolina forty years ago to work at Wilkes Aluminum Company. James recalls, "Back then they were hiring anyone that wanted to work." Most of his income made at Wilkes was spent taking care of his wife and three sons, but, since retiring and moving on his own, James lives comfortably on what he describes as a "nice pension." He has been married twenty-seven years but has been separated from his wife for the past fourteen. He explains, "Me and my wife just grew apart." Two of his three children, all of whom are adults, have been a disappointment to him; they graduated from high school and work odd jobs. His oldest son, however, is a source of pride. James often sticks out his chest, smiles broadly, and says, "My oldest is a career soldier making something of himself." James graduated only high school but attends college courses at one of the local community colleges for his own "self-enhancement." He is frequently excited to talk to willing listeners about things he learns in his Egyptology class.

James hangs out at the tavern, chain-smoking and sipping Heineken beer from a glass of ice. He is low key, but, when he speaks, he often says something the other patrons find worth hearing. He holds patrons' attention as he articulates his theory about issues such as, "our kids' poor education" or "Whites' racist attitudes toward Blacks." James acknowledges that his and other patrons' economic success came as a result of the opportunities Blacks experienced between World War II and the civil rights movement of the 1960s.[4] He is proud of his success and talks about it from time to time with his good friend Thompson, another regular.

Thompson is about James's age, but, unlike James, he refuses to accept the "senior" role. He is a smooth-talking and -walking "slickster" from Atlanta. Before retiring, he spent twenty-five years working for Wilkes Aluminum Company, where he met James. Thompson, forever wanting to maintain his youthful appearance, keeps his head shaved to hide his gray hair and his balding. To those who tease him about being bald, he responds, "Women think baldheaded men are sexy. Just ask Michael Jordan." His haircut gives him the look of a forty-year-old who can hang with the young crowd. Occasionally, Thompson brings one of his "young"—fifty-year-old—girlfriends to the tavern to show her off to the regulars. He struts into the tavern wearing one of his trademark outfits—polyester slacks, expensive leather loafers, and a silk shirt. He accents his outfit with a stylish Kangol cap. When he arrives with a lady friend, he escorts her to the end of the bar without speaking to the other guys. After a few minutes with his lady he takes a seat next to his "boys," who praise him for bringing another "cutey" to the tavern and suggest that "he is the man."

Trena's is a second home to Thompson. His identity is so tied to Trena's social scene that he tells his new acquaintances, "If you can't reach me at Trena's, then try calling me at home. But you're more likely to catch me here." As a single man, he brags to the married patrons that he lives the good life. He has no children and no other serious commitments. With so much free time, Thompson spends several of his weekdays sipping gin and tonic or beer from a tall glass of ice. When he's not at the tavern, by his own account he is either chasing women or washing his car.

David, one of the younger regulars at age thirty-nine, is tall, well built, and, according to Monique, "damn handsome." He works as a professional painter, doing indoor and outdoor paint jobs for a variety of homes and businesses in Chicago and in suburban areas. He is a native Chicagoan, but he, his wife, and their two teenage daughters, Aleece and Asenith, moved to the south suburbs three years ago so that his daughters could attend a suburban public high school because "the high schools in Chicago ain't shit." David frequently talks about how beautiful his daughters are and how he warns them to stay away from most men "'cause they just ain't no good." As far as David is concerned, his daughters belong to him until they turn eighteen, "'cause ain't no teenage daughter of mine goin' be fuckin' 'til she can live on her own."

After work, David drives his late 1980s Leisure Van to the tavern. Entering the tavern in his white dungarees, he spends most of his visits drinking "Bud," smoking cigarettes, flirting with Monique, or watching television. David is an avid fan of daytime soap operas. If he has anything to do with what the patrons will watch on television, it will be the soap operas. *All My Children* and *One Life to Live* are his favorite programs. He became familiar with them several years ago when he was unemployed.

"I didn't have a job, so after I went out looking for work in the morning, I spent my afternoons watching the soaps," explains David. He and Monique often spend time catching up on the soaps and talking about how they expect certain story lines to unfold.

Like David, Hardy is also one of the younger patrons. He is a forty-year-old store manager for a retail chain in Chicago. He works flexible hours and spends much of his free time "chilling" in Trena's. He is a flashy dresser who wears the latest fashion slacks, silk shirts, and eye wear. His outfits are usually accented by gold rings on his fingers and a gold chain around his neck. In fact, the first time I met Hardy, he was decked out in expensive purple slacks and shirt. His attire fits right in with his "smooth" late-model Ford sedan. From time to time, Hardy sits at the tavern sipping his beer and making calls on his cellular phone. He is single and has one son in his twenties that "ain't doing shit but sitting around the house."

Even with his stable employment, Hardy looks for ways to hustle a few extra dollars. He has tried to sell patrons everything from cellular phone service to household products. Occasionally, Hardy pushes his hustle too hard and disrupts the pleasant social atmosphere in the tavern. One day he tried to get a female patron to purchase a phone service he was selling. After several of his attempts, she turned to him and shouted, "I don't wanna be a part of no damn pyramid scheme, so just stop trying to sell it to me. I done spent $1,200 on shit like that before." A hush fell over the tavern, but Hardy, in his typical style, smoothly apologized and "played it off." His ability to shake the female patron's rejection has to do with the fact that other patrons respect Hardy as a man well informed about contemporary social issues. Some patrons even refer to him as Reverend Hardy, fully recognizing his ability to "preach" about social issues.

As one of the few female patrons to visit Trena's, Louise is unique. She is a thirty-four-year-old, fair-complexioned, tall woman the men describe as "thick"—nicely proportioned, but overweight. Her chunky face is highlighted by the red lipstick she wears. Louise is one of Monique's few female friends who comes to Trena's once or twice a week. She sits at the corner of the bar drinking a Miller's Genuine Draft and dragging on her Kool Menthols. Louise works as a dental assistant at Johns Associates, a dental office near Trena's. Yet Monique has suggested that all Louise really does is "just fuck her boss. That's all she does. That's why she be in here all the time. He give her time off work for fucking him." Louise acknowledges that she has "messed around with her boss." As a single woman, she "don't see nothing wrong with that." For the male patrons, Louise is another women to bring into their games of sexual innuendo. She is quite adept at the flirtatious games, skillfully alternating between accepting and rejecting playful sexual overtures from the regulars.

Games of sexual innuendo are enjoyed by both "experienced" and "inexperienced" patrons alike. Pasta is one such "inexperienced" patron. He is a twenty-eight-year-old electrician. Everyone calls him Pasta, a nickname he was given as a child. I remember once asking him his real name, and he responded in a firm voice, "Everyone just calls me Pasta. That's my name." He is originally from Jamaica and moved to Chicago with his parents when he was fourteen years old.

"My people left because they were trying to find work," Pasta explains. He went to high school at one of the "rougher" schools on the south side of Chicago. After he graduated, he worked odd jobs, painting, washing windows, and cleaning. Dissatisfied with his "situation," he entered trade school and learned to be an electrician. He now works with contractors installing electrical wiring in homes and small businesses throughout Chicago.

Although Pasta is single, he always talks about his girlfriend. He spends time having fun with the other patrons by participating in sex talk and innuendo, but, when he talks about more serious matters of commitment, he believes that his girlfriend is the only woman for him. "We'll get married one day, one day," he says. The regulars treat Pasta like a young man who comes to the tavern to be "schooled," and they set out to school him.

Making Trena's Their Own: Tavern Behavior

Trena's location on Eighth Avenue makes it conspicuous to a variety of people, inviting all that pass to enter. Since Trena's is open to the public, Monique and the regulars use an informal screening process to select the "right crowd," or those they will associate with in the tavern. One means of screening is by locking the Eighth Avenue door. Monique used to lock the door to relax her fears of being robbed, but now she also uses it as an effective means of screening nonregulars in general. Since the regulars know that the Eighth Avenue door is locked, they use the west entrance. On occasion, when there are only a few patrons present, Monique locks the west door also. (She does this not because the tavern is in a high-crime area but out of her own sense of insecurity related to her status as a single parent who lives in a high-crime neighborhood herself.) Under such circumstances, only familiar patrons or those who look decent are given access to Trena's. One is familiar if other patrons know one's name, what one does for a living, and why one comes to Trena's. When regulars drive into the tavern parking lot or walk to the door, those inside give shouts of familiarity like, "Here comes Thompson," indicating that the individual outside should be welcomed. If an approaching person is unfamiliar to those inside, then the patrons judge the visitor on appearance.[5] Visitors must look decent. They may convey their decency through three types of symbols: (1) the kind of professional clothing they wear (usually a coat and tie for men or a work uniform); (2) the kinds of cars they drive (any kind of car as long as it does not have custom extras); and (3) by the retired appearance they convey (usually age and type of casual clothing—typically polyester shirts and slacks that flare at the legs). Possession of any of these initial symbols is frequently enough for the individual to gain access to the tavern.

If the approaching individual fails the requisite familiarity or decency test, the door remains locked. Patrons and bartender alike hope that the individual will assume the tavern is closed and depart. Sometimes strangers leave, but on occasion—for example, my first visit to Trena's—individuals knock on the door and are allowed in. If the stranger enters the tavern, the regulars are on warning to keep an eye on the visitor until they know what the stranger is all about. For example, on one occasion two roughly dressed, unkempt men came to the lounge to peddle brand-new CDs and tapes. There were several patrons in the tavern during this time, so Monique had not locked the door. The men entered the tavern and asked patrons to buy their goods. The patrons were visibly apprehensive about the men's presence and rejected their sales pitch. As the strangers left, Monique walked to the door and locked it behind them. She then turned to us and said, "Don't get scared, y'all. I ain't gettin' ready to do nothin' crazy to y'all just 'cause I locked the door. I locked it just to be on the safe side." For Monique, being on the safe side means locking the door to protect herself and patrons from "weird," "strange," or "thug-type" people.

Another means by which Monique and the owner regulate the type of patron that enters the tavern is by establishing and selectively enforcing dress codes. I discovered this after I had been frequenting Trena's for several months, usually wearing blue jeans, a T-shirt, and a baseball cap. On one visit, I was surprised to see a sign posted on the door of Trena's that read, "Men No caps, No gym shoes." I entered the tavern and asked Monique whether I could still come in dressed in my regular clothing. She told me that the sign had been put up for the evening crowd, "not for y'all." The evening hours at Trena's attract a crowd of young men who come to the lounge wearing caps "cocked" to the right or the left. Wearing caps in this way often causes trouble in Trena's because it is a way of showing gang affiliation.[6] Since Trena's cannot legally prohibit people of age from entering the tavern, it institutes rules to constrain activity that is potentially troublesome.

The secure atmosphere and the familiarity among the patrons makes Trena's a second home for many. The regulars receive personal calls on the tavern phone line, watch television as if they were in their own living rooms, and take meals into the tavern to eat. They treat Monique like a personal messenger, leaving detailed messages for her to deliver to other patrons. On Friday afternoons, Monique orders soul food or brings it from home for the after-work happy hour. This means patrons can spend several hours right after work eating home cookin', socializing, and drinking at Trena's. Some have joked that the only reason they go home to sleep after a long party is that "Trena's doesn't have any beds."

Much of the time the regulars spend in Trena's is spent talking about a variety of topics. Some of the patrons' discussions are thoughtful considerations of contemporary issues, while other discussions are comical. For patrons of Trena's, as for individuals in other homogeneous social settings, the quality of conversation is not always based on what is said but can be based on how and who says it. Whether the topics are serious or comical, patrons emphasize a stylized expression typical of neighborhood taverns. This type of stylized talk has been identified as "talking shit."[7] Individuals in Trena's exchange ideas, stories, and jokes, embellishing them with a performance style intended to keep others focused on the presentation. Maintaining others' attention is an important part of social life at Trena's. Through their stylized expression of jokes, social commentary, and story-telling, the regulars also share intimate information about themselves with one another. Sharing this personal information makes Trena's a comfortable and familiar place. It is through "talking shit" that unfamiliar individuals become familiar and develop identities as regulars at Trena's.

Monique facilitates the exchange of ideas throughout the tavern. Her presence is important to tavern social interaction because patron communication often flows through her. As Monique moves around the tavern, she gathers topics of discussion from various discussion groups and transports them to other patrons for discussion. She brings news across the bar with a loud question to a distant patron, saying, for example, "Did you hear that? Did you hear what he said over here? He said. . . ." Her question often initiates interaction between patrons who had not previously been in conversation with each other. Monique's role as intermediary helps patrons to break social barriers between them.

Beyond the patrons' sharing of intimate information and talking shit at Trena's, drinking is also an important part of tavern social life. The regulars, in some ways, become identified by their favorite drink. Monique exhibits knowledge of each patron's favorite drinks, sometimes mixing and serving the drink as the patron enters the tavern, although this is not a common practice because it leads to waste if the patron decides to drink something other than his or her usual. Most often, regulars call out to Monique, "Give me the usual" or "You know what I'm having," to which Monique replies, "I gotcha" and then mixes the drink.

The regulars recognize implicit or explicit norms regulating the amount of liquor that they may consume during their visit to the tavern. For them, it is good to drink, "but not too much to mess you up." The patrons disapprove of individuals who get intoxicated and lose control. Regulars rarely overindulge in the consumption of alcohol, since the overall consensus among patrons supports respectable drinking.

Calvin, Triston, and I sat enjoying our drinks. Triston said, "I come out to drink every now and then, but this guy across the hall from me where I live, he stay drunk. He stay drunk on that Seagrams gin." Triston took a sip of his Heineken and continued, "You can ask anybody. I come up here, and when it's all over I'm walking myself outta here. Ain't nobody gotta take me home."

"I like to drink, too. But I don't mess around wit' no whole lotta stuff," Calvin declared.

"Well, I'm too young to mess around with that hard stuff," I interjected.

*"It's okay to drink. But not too much to mess you up," Triston
concluded.*

Calvin and Triston take pride in being able to hold their liquor
and avoid indications of drinking too much. Their expressions of
control over liquor are consistent with those of other Trena's patrons who recognize that drinking should be social and respectable rather than intoxicating to the loss of control. Yet, frequenting a tavern means that regulars must engage in facework
to disavow, both to themselves and to others, the negative
stereotype of an alcoholic.[8]

*Pasta had been in the bar for quite some time and had already
consumed several drinks. As Pasta was about to leave, Webb
shouted across the bar, "Man, I thought you were leaving?"*

*Pasta hadn't heard Webb because he was in a conversation
with Tom. Webb turned to Monique and said, "Get that man
another drink." He pointed to Pasta.*

*"Okay," Monique answered. She walked over to Pasta, tapped
his hand, and then pointed to Webb, saying, "He's buying you
another drink. Whatchu havin'?"*

*Pasta graciously accepted the drink and questioned Monique
jokingly, "What am I, Monique? What am I? An alcoholic or
what?"*

*Webb interrupted, "You ain't a alcoholic. You a drunk. Alco-
holics go to meetings. Drunks drink, do what they gotta do, and
then go home and get some rest." We all laughed.*

Trena's regulars' conception of consuming liquor is consistent
with how other patrons of neighborhood taverns view drinking
alcohol.[9] The fact that Trena's is a tavern that explicitly serves alcoholic beverages does not mean that everyone who enters is expected to drink them. Many patrons do not drink liquor. Since

some patrons are taking a break from work, they are reluctant to drink on someone else's time. In these cases, patrons order a soft drink or juice. There is little stigma attached to consuming non-alcoholic drinks at Trena's unless the patron is one who ordinarily orders alcoholic beverages. In such a case the purchase of nonalcoholic drinks is grounds for a joke.

> When Jerome entered the lounge and had a seat, Monique walked over and said, "So, Jerome, whatchu goin' have?"
>
> "A 7-Up."
>
> Monique, speaking loudly and smiling, said, "I serve whiskey, not Koolaid, so if you wanna drink you come in here. If you want that punk shit, then you have to get outta here. I'm tired of that damn sickness you got. When you goin' get well?"
>
> "Shit, for the money you charging me, I can go and get a fifth of rum and get drunk."
>
> "Yeah. Shit, you could get a six-pack and chill, and it ain't even goin' cost you two dollars," Monique agreed as they both laughed.

Jerome, a regular who usually drinks Asti Spumante, had been advised by his doctor to stay away from alcohol while he was on medication. He had a legitimate reason for not drinking, and this became the basis for a joke on him. This type of teasing, however, is not extended to the regular patrons who normally order nonalcoholic beverages. Patrons recognize that the tavern is not just a place to drink but a place to socialize, and what a person has in his glass is not as important as what he talks about. As one of the regulars put it, "It don't matter what you drink when you come in here to talk and have a good time." After I established rapport with the regulars, I began drinking what I called a "Jerome Special"—7-Up and cranberry juice. I named the drink after Jerome's daily 7-Ups. My Jerome Special was initially the subject of jokes, since I had been ordering Amaretto Stone Sour or Miller's Genuine Draft previously. Eventually, the jokes about my drink subsided, because, as long as I tipped Monique for the drink and the social time and shared in the social life of the tavern, my consumption of nonalcoholic beverages was of little importance.

Within Trena's, the patrons participate in several amusement activities, including playing video games, listening to the jukebox, and watching television. There are two slot-machine video games, which require one-dollar, five-dollar, ten-dollar, or twenty-dollar bills to operate. The money is converted, by the video game, into "points" to be waged. The patrons wage the points and then activate the slot machine. If the player finishes the game with earned points, the slot machine prints out a tape of the winnings that the patron then presents to Monique. She pays the patron from the cash register for the points accumulated. These video games are owned by Tommy, a fifty-year-old White male who owns an amusement company. He periodically comes to Trena's, resets the machines, collects any unawarded cash, and leaves. The intensity with which the patrons become involved in playing the video games varies. Some patrons talk to the video game or involve others in their interaction with the video game.

Bobby was standing at the video game, and he pulled a ten-dollar bill from his wallet and inserted it into the game. He started wagering his points and then talked to the video game. He said, "Come on now. Thirty points. I need thirty points." He pressed the button on the game. Monique watched Bobby as she walked to his side at the video game. Bobby said to the machine, as he rocked it a little, "Now come on." The images on the screen were going around and then began to slow down.

Monique shouted, "OOOoo. You gone get it."

Bobby kept bumping the machine and said, "Come on." As the machine stopped, Bobby shouted, "All right." Bobby waged some more points and played again. As he was playing the game, James walked around to his side.

"I'm coming to bring you luck," James said to Bobby.

"You're fucked now, Bobby," Monique said as she smiled at James.

"I ain't goin' play no more," Bobby said. James sat down on the bar stool next to Bobby and watched him finish his game. When Bobby finished he removed the tape and gave it to Monique. He had won twenty-five dollars. After Monique gave him the cash from the register, Bobby returned to the game and said, "Now I gotta play again."

Monique said to Bobby, "You don't know how to quit."

Music from the jukebox also offers the patrons the opportunity to draw one another into face-to-face interaction. Patrons enjoy listening to music in Trena's. They sing along with some of their favorite tunes as the jukebox plays a variety of popular music, blues, jazz, and "dusties"—music played by Black musicians during the 1950s and 1960s Motown era. Monique sometimes gets into the act.

We were listening to one of Aretha Franklin's—the "Queen of Soul"—older tunes. As the lyrics "If you want a do-right, all-night woman" blared through the jukebox, Monique turned to me to finish the verse with Aretha. She wiggled her waist and sang along, "then you got to be a do-right, all-night man."

Monique adds her own force to the song, positioning her body in an explicit sexual posture and winding her waist. She uses the jukebox to convey her "sexy side."[10] Patrons often pick up on other songs and sing along with them, adding their own twist on familiar lyrics, sometimes changing them to give them new meaning in tavern social life. Even though the jukebox is an important form of amusement for the patrons, there are times when its use is considered a distraction from other activities in the tavern. Patrons most frequently consider jukebox music a distraction when they are attempting to listen to and view television or converse.

Conclusion

I ventured into Trena's with the objective of understanding the regulars' lifestyles and identifying the cultural subtleties that give Trena's its flavor as a middle-class African American social setting. These cultural subtleties become evident in my examination of patrons' feelings about work and family, their thoughts on mass media, their talk concerning race, and their games of sexual innuendo. While taverns like Trena's have been identified primarily as places of fun and play, they are also places where patrons give serious thought to social issues. I examine tavern social interaction in an attempt to unearth ways that patrons' symbolic gestures and exchanges help them make sense of their "real-world" experiences in a "private" domain. An underlying assumption of this approach is that if individual social identities are formed in relation to a multitude of experiences, settings, and interactions with a variety of people and places, then the time that patrons spend with their peers helps them shape the way they view the world around them.

Chapter Two

WORK AND THE TAVERN

There goes the whole day. You ain't done no work yet and you drinking like that."

In my time at the tavern, I learned that the patrons view Trena's as a place where those with "good jobs" congregate. To the regulars, good jobs are not necessarily professional or white-collar jobs but include blue-collar jobs that pay sufficient wages for workers to take care of their families, save a few dollars, and enjoy the good life. The regulars earn their living from a variety of jobs, including postal worker, dental assistant, police officer, painter, electrician, line worker, and corrections officer. Some patrons work in white-collar jobs, as insurance agents, doctors, lawyers, and government employees. Still others are small-time entrepreneurs.

While white-collar and blue-collar jobs are accorded varying prestige outside the tavern, few patrons make distinctions inside the tavern among themselves on the basis of employment. This is due, in large part, to patrons' belief that deeply embedded historical racism and discrimination have negatively impacted African Americans' employment opportunities and class standing. Furthermore, for those socially mobile African Americans who have been able to attain middle-class status despite limited opportunity, *de facto* and *de jure* residential segregation have confined them to areas near the Black urban poor.[1] Unlike socially mobile Whites, middle-class African Americans are unable to put significant social or spatial distance between themselves and their poorer racial kindred. Under these conditions, the lines of class status are blurred as people who live in close proximity to one another come to share some cultural commonalities. The patrons believe that, for an African American, racial status is far more important than social class status. As one patron stated, "Even if you make it, you still just another niggah." Thus, Trena's regulars emphasize few social class distinctions among themselves. As long as a man can maintain a decent living, earn an honest dollar, and effectively participate in story and joke telling, he is welcomed into Trena's as a man of middle-class stature. Additionally, the patrons find maintaining stable employment and successful completion of meaningful work highly desirable. Indeed, none of the patrons was unemployed during my years at the tavern. It is the relationship between patrons' work and their social life that is brought out in everyday interaction within the tavern.

Work and Leisure

Every weekday afternoon, regulars gather at Trena's for leisure. From early afternoon until early evening, there is a steady stream of regulars who pour in and out of Trena's like workers changing shifts, as patrons sometimes tell one another, "Man, get off that stool and go to work; it's my shift at the bar." Like working patrons who frequent other taverns,[2] the regulars have tavern time predetermined by their work schedules. There are three kinds of employment schedules for the regulars of Trena's. The first is the time regulated by the traditional eight-hour workday. Patrons who are, for example, government employees work this schedule and usually join the other members of the tavern after work. Members of this group have the least amount of flexibility in determining when they can make it to the tavern to relax, although a few can choose to have a late lunch so that they may "dip" into the tavern for a soft drink and a bit of early afternoon talk. Other patrons, like manufacturing workers, work unusual shifts (e.g., 7:00 A.M. until 3:30 P.M. or 8:00 P.M. until 4:00 A.M.). They get off work or arrive at the tavern before work to hang out. Still others, such as insurance salesmen, work jobs where they control the time they arrive at the tavern. Much of their work is done at home or in the field, and they determine when they will meet clients, finish reports, or check into the office. Despite the disparity in work schedules most of the regulars generally "hit" the tavern between 2:30 P.M. and 5:30 P.M.

Monique and the patrons are keenly aware of work schedules. Patrons' work becomes intertwined with the social life of the tavern in such a way that others know the time and the day that most patrons can come into the tavern. If a patron should appear before his usual time, he is interrogated, because to the regulars work is serious and should be honored. The men will often joke with a delinquent worker, "You ain't supposed to be in here. Get your ass to work." Through their teasing and questioning, the patrons help to maintain the integrity of the tavern as a place where working men come to hang out. For Monique, working customers are good to have around because "they can leave you a fuckin' tip." For the patrons, having others around who work gives them other people who can relate to work experience, that is, what it feels like to have "the boss on your ass" or to "get the job done."

Work and Social Status

Some of the patrons' employment and education backgrounds indicate a blue-collar or working-class status. Yet, I classify the tavern as a middle-class social space because the patrons' overall work experiences, educational backgrounds, and lifestyle are grounded in middle-class values and ideals.[3] They share the traditional middle-class value of developing a career, rather than just "holdin' onto a job." They feel that work precedes fun and play and that education is an important means for becoming someone in America. Some of these men have college degrees and advanced professional degrees. To them, education is so important that they express particular disappointment if their children have failed to take advantage of educational opportunity. As one patron put it, "I can't stand it when my son just sits around and does Jack Shit. He's got to go out and get his education and get a damn job." In addition to their beliefs about work and education, patrons share middle-class expectations that leisure time should be spent traveling to "exotic" places and entertaining oneself with all of the latest mass consumer products, such as big-screen televisions, camcorders, DVD systems, computers, and satellite dishes.

Distinctions between middle- and working-class status are further clouded by the patrons' belief that overt racism in the job market at the time they were first active in the labor force meant that many college-trained African Americans were forced to take jobs as store clerks, garbage collectors, secretaries, or other menial positions. "Shit, we couldn't get a better job if we went to college back then, anyway," one patron observed. Through the process of racial exclusion, some jobs traditionally identified by Whites as working class took on middle-class status in African American communities; therefore, the patrons generally recognize one another as middle class even though some were employed in jobs traditionally associated with the working class. In short, patrons broadly define as middle class those folks who have some postsecondary education, work a legitimate job with steady income, are able to get credit and purchase consumer items, enjoy an occasional vacation to a Caribbean island, come to the tavern for leisure activity, and party from time to time without missing a bill payment.[4]

Much like members of other racial and ethnic middle-class groups, Trena's patrons try to enjoy the leisure activities associated with "having a little dough." They enjoy the hottest trends and expensive vacations out of a sense of entitlement, as Ricky, a carpenter, points out.

Ricky had been away from the tavern a few days and then came back. His skin was noticeably darker than when he left. When Ricky came into the tavern, Monique commented, "Boy, you look like you been out there in the sun."

"Shit, yeah," he replied. "I went down to Jamaica for four days and three nights. Me and my lady went to chill. I needed to get away and have a good time."

"I bet that was nice?"

"Yeah. The hotel was right on the beach, and they set you up with all the food you can eat and all the drinks you want. I was kickin' back and sippin' in the sun," he laughed.

"That must have cost some good money?"

"Yeah, but I work, and I got a little money, so I'ma spend it doing shit I like to do. Money ain't no good if you don't spend it sometimes. As long as I can take care of my regular expenses, I

don't give a shit about how much something cost. I'ma have a
good time 'cause I work for it."

Patrons like Ricky enjoy some of life's luxuries, yet they also
recognize that the "good life" is fragile and suffers with changing times.

Changing Times and Work

"Man, Black folks had it made," Mickey, a machinist, once com-
mented.
"Shit. When I was coming up that's just when we started get-
ting the chance to make something out of ourselves. We had
opportunity, and we had choices. Lots of us started working then."

Mickey's words relate to the ways in which major economic
and political changes have resulted in the expansion of the Black
middle class over the past twenty years.[5] Many African Americans, like Mickey, fought for and benefited from affirmative action, improved educational training, equal employment, and
growth in the American economy. These major changes significantly shaped the social position of a number of patrons, who
moved into the labor force at a time when social pressures created massive opportunities. And yet, many patrons pessimisti-
cally point out that the lifestyles they have enjoyed will no
longer be available to younger African Americans.

Leroy and Spice had been talking, when Leroy finished his
drink and left, Spice turned to me.
"We all retired," he said, pointing to Thompson and James.
"We got up this morning and had breakfast, and now we just
hanging around here. We do it at least one day a week."

"So this is like a ritual thing for y'all?" I asked.

"Yeah. It's just a little something we do." I picked up my drink and moved to the seat next to him.

"We worked for Wilkes Aluminum Company," he continued. "I worked there thirty-eight years and nine months and was able to retire."

"That's a long time."

"Yeah, when I first started working for the company I made a dollar forty-six an hour, and that was enough to pay for the things I wanted."

"What? The only thing you coulda wanted then was a pack of cigarettes," I said, and we both laughed. "Did y'all have a union?" I asked.

"Yeah, we had a union. We went through six or seven strikes to get all the stuff we got today. The White workers wasn't really interested in our help during the strikes, either. They really wanted us to get the fuck out. But we had to keep fightin'. I figured I'd keep trying to get the benefits. Hell, I had fought in a war, so I figured I deserved the benefits of a good life. See, after I served in the Korean War from '51 to '53, I went right to work for Wilkes."

"So what did you do at Wilkes?"

"I had to learn how to use a lot of different tools at the plant."

"Did you get job training before you started?"

"Job training? Hell, naw. Back then everybody was taught how to use the tools right on the job, none of this job training shit where you have to spend all of your money. . . . But I understand that times are different now, and technology means that you need more training. So y'all young folks gotta stay in school 'cause there ain't gon' be no more jobs like the ones we had making sixteen or seventeen dollars an hour. We had it made."

Spice reached into his pocket and showed me his union membership card. "I had a good work life. My parents and their par-

ents, they didn't have it so good. Shit, when we got our jobs at Wilkes, we got all the health benefits and everything. Just look at me." He jumped off the bar stool, stood up, and flexed his muscles.

"I'm strong and healthy. My grandparents would be sixty-six, and they would move around slowly talkin' about, 'Sonny could you pass me a chair, or go get me this or that?' But it's different for us. We have fun. Shit, I got two women, one that's twenty-eight, and one that's forty-three. All I gotta do is cut my grass and chase after young pussy."

We laughed.

Spice suggests his life was transformed by the massive changes in work conditions for African Americans, especially during the migration of Blacks from the rural South to the industrial North from the 1900s to the 1960s.[6] Having worked and built up a retirement fund, Spice and his friends enjoy a life of leisure. Spice recognizes the constraints on his grandparents and the constraints soon to come on the generation after him. "It will be tough for younger generations to live like we live," he said. Patrons who currently work admit that they struggle even now. They remain keenly aware of the changing conditions of a globalized economy in America and how those conditions will continue to affect the value of what they earn at work.[7] The patrons' understanding comes through time and again in their reminiscent stories, like this discussion between William and Aaron regarding the value of a hundred dollars.

William said, "The first time I ate pussy it was Ms. Carroll. She was older than I was. Shit. She pushed my head down between her legs and handed me a hundred-dollar bill. Now, you know, I remember a hundred-dollar bill 'cause it was a whole lot of money then. Shit, it would probably be worth ten thousand dollars today." We laughed.

Aaron turned and added, "You know, back when I got married, one hundred dollars was a lot of money. I got married in '54. Shit, I used to work for United Airlines making fifty-six dollars a week. I had a wife and two kids and could come home and pay the rent, give her some money, and still have some money left over. I could go to the bar and have a drink, or I could get me a little hotel room if I needed to."

"You right about that," William said.

"Shit, I'm making seven hundred dollars a week now and don't have enough money for shit," Aaron said.

"I know what you talking about," I said.

Aaron called to Brene, the bartender covering for Monique, "Come on, fix me one more drink. I decided I'ma leave at 6:00."

He got up and walked back to the middle of the bar while Brene fixed him a Bloody Mary. He said to Brene, "Now, you know, I ain't got no mo' money today."

"Don't worry about it. You good," Brene said.

William and Aaron recognize that their hard-earned money has less value today than in the past. Even though the patrons talk about having money trouble, bartenders do not hesitate to extend drink credit to them, since they are men who have a history of work and have developed the reputation as "folks that pay what they owe ya." In fact, Monique and the other bartenders frequently practice a "drink now and pay later" policy. Most of the men return later in the afternoon to square away debts; still others pay on the following day.

Work and Privilege

The frequency with which the men visit the tavern suggests that, for this group of men, there is a logical fit between work and the tavern. As Nelson, a Cook County sheriff, and Duke, a construction worker, both in their fifties, point out, patrons take their work as a proud privilege and their social life in the tavern as a reward for their hard work.

> I was at the bar sipping my drink, and I overheard Duke and Nelson talking about hanging out at Trena's. I turned to Duke and asked, "Man, I see you in here a lot. How often are you in here?"
>
> "Every day," he responded.
>
> "Damn," I said. "I can't even hang. I'd be dead."
>
> "Shit, we be in here every day 'cause we ain't got to worry about shit. We working hard at work, and we've already outlived the critics."
>
> Nelson and Duke slapped hands together in agreement as Nelson added, "That's right. We outlived the life expectancy for the Black man. We can smoke, drink, take drugs, whatever. . . . I know I ain't leaving nothing for my family. They goin' be at my funeral puttin' dirt on my grave and saying, 'Damn, daddy was a nice man, but he didn't leave us shit.'" We laughed.

Since patrons think of the tavern as a place of rest, it is often the first place to turn to after leaving work. In fact, for some the tavern is the perfect place to escape the rigors of the "real world," including the family.

> Sam walked into the tavern and moved steadily to the bar. Monique approached him and asked, "Did you just get off work?"
>
> "Yeah," he sighed.
>
> "Well, I only got three more hours, and then I'm off," Monique responded. "Whatcha having?"
>
> "A Miller's. I gotta relax. Shit, I already put in ten hours."
>
> "I know you're glad to be off."
>
> "Yeah. I gotta take a break before I go home to the family. I can't go walking through the door and hear my wife nagging me about some shit after I done had to deal with White folks telling

me what to do all day and how to do it. I need a break in the worst way." Monique and Sam laughed.

"Well, you're in the right place," Monique responded.

Sam, like so many other patrons who work during the early morning hours, spends the late afternoon hours relaxing from his job as a mechanic. Unlike Sam, whose job requires him to be physically present, other regulars have more flexible hours and can escape work sooner than Sam. The patrons are also free to break from the constraints of the office and the constant control that White managers and supervisors have over their time and work. From time to time, these regulars slip into the tavern for an early afternoon break. Some even bring their office work to the tavern.

The soap opera One Life to Live *had just concluded, and the tabloid news program* Inside Edition *was beginning. At the same time, Terrence had selected the Toni Braxton CD from the jukebox. As the jukebox and television were playing, Wallace sat reviewing insurance policies he secured for the day. After a few minutes of this, he turned to Monique and said, "Well, I got that done. I think I'ma just cool out the rest of the day. It's too nice of a day to be up in that office listening to my White supervisor complain about something or another."*

"Yes, it's a beautiful day," Monique replied.

"Yeah. That's what I'll do. I'll finish my drink, leave here, go to the bank, head on out to the Best Western, and then go on to the house."

Monique smiled at Wallace and said, "I know what you up to. I guess you got it like that. You can work where you play, drink where you work, and then go mess around." We laughed.

The mixture of white-collar and blue-collar jobs with flexible hours means that the regulars who enter the tavern in the early afternoon are privileged. They have the ability to determine when they will work and how much they work. Sometimes the men are only taking a break from work, in which case they order a soft drink; however, if a regular comes in and orders hard liquor, it is his way of signaling to all present that he is claiming his own time and that he no longer "owes time to the gig" or "wanna worry about what White folks are doing."

Tony came in at around 2:00 P.M. He sat down and waited for Monique to get to his side of the bar. "Give me a Martell," he demanded.

Pasta, who was taking a break from work, turned to Tony. "Shit. There goes the whole day. You ain't done no work yet, and you drinking like that. There goes the whole Goddamn day."

"I finished my work, and so you're right, there goes the whole damn day. I'm relaxin'. See, I got my work done, the boss is satisfied, and now it's time for me to chill. I'm not trying to sit up in here and worry about all of the problems of the world or what White folks are doing. I'm chilling."

"I heard that," Pasta replied with a smile.

The patrons hold their place of employment high. They give work such esteem because they recognize the consequences of a shifting economy, massive downsizing, and the closing off of traditional jobs in favor of more technical jobs as a significant transformation of the contemporary work world. Thus, despite the nation's overall economic prosperity in the 1990s, the patrons believe it to be increasingly difficult to get a "good job" and maintain it.

On television, the newscaster began discussing a decline in the U.S. economy. Nick turned to Ricky and Andre and said, "Things is bad all over."

"Yeah," Andre said in agreement.

"There are people just starting out that have to wait two weeks to be able to pay their rent," Nick continued. "Even some of the doctors are starting out bad."

"Yeah, but with the money they making, they can at least get a little apartment," Ricky said.

"Shit, they better be making some real money. Rent, your security deposit, that's as much as a down payment on a damn house. You also gotta understand that a lot of those doctors have gotten student loans to get through medical school. And don't think about buying a car. You die trying to pay rent and a car note," Nick said.

"Yeah, you're right about that. They had done a study, and it found that the average person spends thirty-one weeks of their salary on a car," Andre added.

"That's a lot of money," Ricky said.

"Oh, yeah," Nick shouted, "it's bad. They got truck drivers taking cuts just so they can keep their jobs. And they already ain't making nothing but nine dollars an hour. I don't know how folks goin' be able to live after a while. And, you know, if everybody else is suffering, then you know the brothers are hurtin' more."

Consistent with the patrons' recognition that times are bad for many Americans, and yet worse for African Americans, is the fact that past discrimination has caused African Americans to suffer measurably. Even the Black middle class has endured inequity in income, education, and wealth when compared to Whites of similar social standing.[8]

Unemployment

Despite the overall resurgence of the American economy, African Americans remain at a distinct disadvantage when compared to Whites.[9] Not surprisingly, given the fact that a greater proportion of African Americans are unemployed than are Whites, many of the patrons within the tavern have family or friends who are also unemployed. In fact, college-educated members of the Black middle class have a 20 percent chance of coming in contact with someone in their neighborhood who is receiving welfare, whereas college-educated Whites have only an 8 percent chance.[10] Even within the tavern, the patrons cannot escape the reality of unemployment for many of their contemporaries.

After playing the game, Tray went and sat at his seat by the opening in the bar. Carol, a woman whom I had not seen before, walked hurriedly into the tavern. She was dark skinned, with a ponytail in her hair, busty, and overweight. She appeared to be in her late twenties and wore an aqua-green sweatsuit and a bowling league jacket. When she came in, Tray said to her in a surprised voice, "Hey, Carol, what's up?"

"Nothing baby, I'm hustling. I'm back on the yard [south side of Chicago] now. You gone see me around. I'm trying to get a job," Carol said.

"Weren't you working for the Rainbow Candy Company?"

"Yeah, but they started letting people go. Now I'm looking for a job, and I'm still in school, too. I got about two more years left 'cause I refuse to take out any more student loans. I'm about to be married next month, so I got to get a job."

Monique and Betty were setting up for a big party that would take place later that evening. When Carol finished her discussion with Tray, she turned to Betty and asked, "Do you have an application?"

Monique pointed to the cash register and told Betty, "Look for the applications back behind the cash register." Betty fumbled around, and she finally found one, "Got it." She handed the application to Carol.

"Do you have any experience working in a bar?" Monique asked Carol.

"Yeah," Carol replied. "I opened Onyx, I opened Clarence's, and I opened up the Tiger Lounge; then I took a job in a restaurant for a little while. I worked at the Tiki Lounge after that for the last three years." Carol then sat down and filled out the application. After completing the application Carol handed it to Betty and said eagerly, "Okay, who do I talk to?"

"The owner is not in right now, but she usually gets in about seven," Betty responded. "I'll give it to her and let her call you."

"Thank you," Carol said as she headed for the door. She turned to Tray and said, "Well, I'm on the yard again. You'll see me around. Bye."

"See ya," Tray said. As Carol left, Tray shook his head from side to side and said, "Damn, man, that's rough. She had a good job, and it's gone, just like that."

The regulars talk about the difficulties of competing for jobs that would sustain a living for those who are heads of households. They share a realization that jobs are hard to come by even for those with skills and ability that fit the needs of the employer. In Carol's case, she applied for a job at the tavern for which she had much experience but ultimately was not hired since the tavern was fully staffed. Given the lack of predictable future job opportunities, many patrons continue to hold onto their current jobs, even when they feel they might experience immediate financial gain from a shift in employment.[11] As one patron, restating the old cliche, said, "A job in the hand is worth two in the bush."

While all of the regulars are employed or retired and feel strongly that men who can work should work, there are occasions when the men also perceive unemployment as acceptable. For instance, those in apprentice or trade school programs or a student like myself had an acceptable stint of unemployment. As a graduate student with a family, I sometimes felt the financial strains of working only part-time. There were many days when both Monique and the other patrons would offer words of encouragement after I had complained about my financial situation. Monique once said, "Ain't nothing wrong with you not having a job right now. You in school working. You'll get the real job when you get done." When I complained to Charles one day about not having money and struggling, he said, "Well, you gettin' yo' Ph.D. That's something special. You can work after you finish school." Several patrons would commend me for my hard work in school in much the same way the men of Jelly's praised Anderson.[12] For the patrons, those individuals who are working to improve their overall social position by forgoing work for school are looked on with favor.

Work and Its Resources

Beyond the symbolic aspect of conversations about work, there is the practical side to work talk. Trena's regulars have "real jobs" where they do tasks using skills developed through years of employment. Patrons bring this wealth of knowledge to others within the tavern, making the tavern not only a place to relax and share stories with one's peers but a place where practical information can be exchanged. I found myself learning from the patrons' work talk with one another. For instance, Pasta, an electrician, and Shorty, his twenty-two-year-old assistant, share practical information with Jack, an insurance salesman.

Jack had been sitting at the bar having a drink when his buddy Gerald left. Jack turned to Monique and said, "Give me one more for the road, like them fellas over there." He pointed to Pasta and

Shorty and added, "I'm on the same highway they on, and I ain't coming off 'til they get off. I'm comin' off at the ramp they come off." Jack's statement caught Pasta's attention. Pasta laughed and raised his glass to Jack.

Shorty, who had been waiting for Pasta to finish his drink so that they could leave, started to plead with Pasta, "Come on, man. Can we go?" Pasta stood up and said, "Monique, sweetheart, let me paya 'cause I gotta go. I gotta get back to work."

"Hey, wait before you go," Jack shouted to Pasta. "I got a question. I put in a three-way switch in my house, but it don't work from both sides. I gotta cut it off upstairs, but I gotta go downstairs to cut it on. Now, what did I do wrong?"

Pasta sat contemplating Jack's question. He stood up and said to Jack, "Repeat it."

"I put in a three-way switch, but it don't work from both sides. What did I hook up wrong?"

"You probably put the three switch in on the travel wire."

"What did I do?" Jack asked again.

"You musta put the travel switch in the wrong place."

"Yeah, he put the travel switch in the wrong place," Shorty interjected.

Pasta's electronic pager started to beep. He looked down at it and then turned to Shorty and said, "Draw it up so he can see what we talking about. I'm goin' to make this phone call." Pasta walked to the pay phone.

Shorty asked Monique for a pen. She moved to get the pen. Jack jokingly shouted, "Shorty, hurry up. I bet you don't move this slow when some girl talkin' about giving you some pussy." Shorty and Monique laughed. Jack added, "Whatcha need, a pen? I got one." Shorty walked over to Jack and started drawing the diagram on a napkin.

After Pasta finished his phone call, he walked over to Jack and Shorty. Pasta said to Shorty, "And you better be drawing it

right." After showing Jack how to fix his electrical problem,
they briefly exchanged pleasantries, and then Pasta and Shorty
departed.

One of the interesting things about these kinds of exchanges
between the patrons is that the regulars share their practical resources with those around them without the expectation that
they receive immediate compensation in return. Instead, reciprocity of information is achieved over time. As patrons go out
into the work world every day, they encounter a number of daily
experiences that may later prove useful to others within the tavern. They return to the tavern with the ability to spread this information, whether as an attorney clarifying some aspect of the
law, a city worker explaining how to avoid "red tape," an insurance salesman illuminating the advantages of particular policies,
or a businessman describing ways to secure a loan. Their exchanges move the tavern beyond a place of fun and play to a
place of ever-evolving practical information.

Although the regulars are willing to freely exchange information, they are much less likely to do any of the actual work
for free. Ken, a handyman, conveys this sentiment.

The telephone had been ringing quite a bit this afternoon. This
was a problem for Monique, since the connection in the front was
screwed up. She could barely hear the telephone ring, and that
meant once she did hear it, she had to run into the back room just
to answer it. As Ken and Bob sat next to me drinking beer, the
telephone rang and both Bob and I shouted to Monique down at
the north end of the bar. As she ran down the bar to the back
room, she said, "I'm sick of this phone ringing, 'cause every damn
time it rings I gotta run my ass all the way to the back."

After she got off the telephone Bob said, "Why don't Terrence
and Trena fix the phone?"

Monique said, "They did, but people walk on the carpet, and it keeps shorting it out."

Then Bob turned to Ken, a self-proclaimed fix-it man, and asked, "Ken, why don't you fix it for them? You could hook it up for them so it would work. Then Monique wouldn't have to run back and forth."

"Shit. I won't fix nothing else in here. I fixed the cash register, and Terrence didn't even give me a drink. I ain't fixing nothing in here," Ken replied.

Then Bob said, "Yeah, I fixed that box back there for Terrence, and all he gave me was a drink. Now I know that if I had gone out to somebody's house and fixed it, I woulda got at least fifty dollars. All he goin' give me is a drink. Now, Trena, she paid me when I fixed that furnace. But it still ain't enough."

The regulars are more than willing to share information about how to repair equipment, but less likely to do the actual work for others. Patrons avoid working for others because it could complicate the relationships that currently exist. For instance, if asked to do work by another patron, few of the men would propose up front a price for their work, leaving just compensation up to the discretion of those requesting the favor. This ultimately becomes problematic since the giver operates under the expectation of some unknown amount of cash payment, while the receiver operates under the assumption that the work is a favor. If, for example, Pasta had actually repaired Jack's electrical circuit in his home, Pasta's work might have been perceived by Jack as a favor between friends, while Pasta might have expected compensation for the expenditure of his valuable time. To avoid such a situation, the regulars opt to spend their extra time in leisure with one another, rather than complicating their relationships with the formalities brought on by "business."

Another benefit of patrons' work to the tavern social atmosphere is that patrons who have jobs where promotional items are given away or where "surplus" stock—at least from the employees' perspective—is available bring these items into the tavern and distribute them among the patrons. Occasionally, Steve, a thirty-five-year-old bakery delivery driver, brings day-old donuts from the bakery where he works, while Moe, who works for a potato chip company, regularly brings "surplus" bags of chips to give to the bartenders to share with the other patrons.

We had been sitting in the tavern for a little while now, and the man across the bar asked Yolanda, "Y'all got anything to eat around here?"

Then Moe said to Yolanda, "What happened to your chips? You should give your customers some."

Yolanda went under the counter and got the customer some cheese popcorn. Moe then asked me, "You want some popcorn?"

I said, "Yeah." Yolanda gave me a bag and then distributed the other bags underneath the counter around the bar.

Moe said, "See, people don't believe me that when you give a customer something, that make him feel guilty about tipping. They'll leave you a little extra money if they get something free."

I laughed, and Moe turned to me and said, "I'm serious."

"I know," I replied. "When I worked as a waiter and I gave a little extra sauce or something like that for people, it always seemed like they tipped more."

"See, if they get something from you," Moe continued, "instead of tipping you fifty cents they might tip you a dollar."

Yolanda interrupted, "You know why I didn't pass them out? 'Cause you remember yesterday when they asked you for some more chips and you gave them some? Well, they had already had some chips, and they was just playing like that hadn't had any so you would give them some more."

Moe said, "You know what? I knew they already had some. But you know why I gave them some more? 'Cause all the night shift do at my job is take the chips in the back and put them up until they leave for home and then they take 'em home. So I'd rather just share 'em with y'all."

While some patrons share food items, those who work for law firms or for the city can obtain higher-status items like corporate tickets to professional sporting events, including Chicago Bulls basketball games or White Sox and Cubs baseball games. Thus, the patrons' range of occupations provides a range of benefits to those within the tavern. Such sharing of chips and donuts or tickets to sporting events is symbolic of the patrons' general attitude, as expressed by Charles: "If I got something my boys can use, I'ma share it." The patrons' work status provides the resources to share.

Conclusion

Patrons' work is significant to the social life of the tavern because it provides a common thread for social interaction among the patrons, a source of individual legitimacy, and concrete and abstract resources for the regulars. Unlike some patrons of taverns in low-income neighborhoods, Trena's patrons share a vision of work as a source of importance.[13] They honor their individual work and respect one another because each patron recognizes the challenge of maintaining steady employment. Despite the emphasis on work, patrons are also careful not to overemphasize the importance of particular kinds of occupations. Their reluctance results in part from their recognition that historical racial discrimination forced Blacks with higher qualifications to accept traditionally lower-status jobs than merited by their credentials; therefore, the men see the commonality of race, age, and culture of struggle as African American men as providing far greater cohesion for them than occupational status. To the patrons, a Black man who has "outlived the critiques," "holds a decent job," and "takes care of business" is one worthy of association, no matter the occupation.

Chapter Three

TELEVISION INTERACTION AND RACE

How a Black man goin' have his woman taken from him by a White boy? He stupid for being on TV with that mess anyway.

Before I began my research at Trena's, I had found myself intrigued with the social atmosphere of drinking establishments in general, not because I felt the need to drink alcohol but because I was attracted to the loud clamor of intense social interaction. The drinking place, to me, was a part of the fast-paced city life from which I hailed. I longed to be involved in the broad range of social games and activities in the drinking spots that had appeal to me. Dancing, throwing darts, playing video games, and listening to live entertainment all had their redeeming qualities. Yet the activity I found most intriguing in a number of drinking establishments was patrons' use of television. In fact, once I began research at Trena's, I discovered that the patrons, like so many other Americans, enjoy spending their leisure time in the tavern viewing television.

As they sip their drinks and talk shit with their buddies, the regulars sometimes glance at the television, while other times they focus on television as the topic of conversation. During their peak time in the tavern, the patrons most frequently prefer to view programs from the talk show, soap opera, and tabloid "news" genres, which focus on "dirty" sex, "hot" intimacy, "big" scandals, and racial problems.[1] Patrons' focus on programming such as soap operas and talk shows is related to the dialogue format of these television programs. This format, in which television characters exchange dialogue with one another, allows patrons to symbolically participate in the on-screen conversation. Patrons inject their commentary or "put their two cents in" throughout the program. This exchange between patrons and TV personae raises questions regarding the impact of the use and the content of television on life at Trena's. I explore this impact, especially with regard to patrons' discussions of race.

Controlling Television Viewing

At first glance, it appears that Monique, who is the "owner" of the television remote control, is solely responsible for selecting what programs the patrons view, but a closer look reveals that there are various modes of television control, ranging for Monique's direct control to patrons' direct control. Still, Monique is significantly involved in program selection, as demonstrated by her behavior one day in the tavern.

As the patrons started up a conversation, Monique walked back around the bar to the southwest corner and picked up the remote control to the television. She pointed the remote control and turned the channel. The first channel she stopped at was VH1, a music video station. On VH1 there was a video of Anita Baker, who sings rhythm and blues. She was singing her new release, "Body and Soul." As Monique stopped on this channel, the noise in the tavern died down, and the patrons stopped talking.

"Damn, y'all sure' got quiet," Monique said.

"Yeah," I added in agreement. As I turned to the television I said, "She looks different."

"Yeah, she does," Monique replied. "It's her hair."

"Yep. You're right, it is her hair."

After Anita Baker's video ended, the next video began. A White rock band was beginning its song, but as soon as Monique saw the video, she picked up the remote control and turned the television to BET [Black Entertainment Television]. On BET there was a video playing, "This D.J.," by Warren G, a rap artist. Monique said, "Now we can't watch this 'cause I don't like no gangsta rap. I can't watch nobody call nobody a bitch. I hear enough of that from my sisters." [2]

Monique, although acting autonomously, reads the patrons' responses to television programs as a means of understanding their viewing preference. In fact, her changing from a gangsta rap video is a response to the tavern moral order that rejects the youthful ideas associated with gangsta rap and other forms of hip-hop.[3] Occasionally Monique fails to apprehend the patrons' cues of dissatisfaction with programs like rap videos. In such cases, the patrons prompt Monique to recognize their normative standards for viewing and request that she turn the channel or turn the television off altogether.

Moe was looking up at the music video on the screen that was over his head. It was a medium-speed song, with a hip-hop artist singing. Moe turned to Monique and said, "Why don't you turn that video off? Why don't you rent them videos and take them home?"

"This ain't no movie video, that's the TV," Monique said.

"You need to turn it off. Why don't you turn on the box [stereo]?" Moe said.

Monique picked up the remote control to turn off the television as she said, "I can't help it that I like music videos."

"Well, you can't even understand what they saying on there," Moe said.

"Yes, I can."

Moe began mocking the video by making noises and howling sounds, "Mmyyyy wwhhyyy howllll. You can't even understand what they saying."

Monique turned the television to CNN and then walked over to the D.J. booth and played an Anita Baker CD.

Monique's failure to perceive Moe's dissatisfaction with videos is representative of the tension created by the age difference between the patrons and Monique. She is stuck in the world between personal enjoyment and maintaining the relaxed nature of the tavern that serves the needs of the customers. When she fails to observe the patrons' viewing needs, some patrons become impatient and, instead of prompting Monique to change the channel, take control of the television themselves, declaring, "I have seen enough of this." Even though patrons have the power to select the programs, this does not guarantee that their selection will go unchallenged by Monique.

At about this time, Tray, a patron in his early thirties, grabbed the remote control and jokingly said, "It's time for BET videos."

"Wait a minute," Monique said. "My stories are going off in a minute. Don't nobody wanna see no videos, anyway. If you wanna see videos, take yo' ass home." We laughed.

Tray turned the channel as a joke and the first thing he turned to was a talk show that featured three Black men. One was Leon

Isaac Kennedy, an African American movie star from the late 1980s. When Tray turned to this channel, Monique suddenly shouted, "OOooo, Leon Isaac Kennedy. I used to have a crush on him. . . ."

"Oh," Tray interrupted, "we can leave it here 'cause it's something you like."

"Yeah," Monique said with a smile.

Monique's original challenge follows the consensus viewing habits among the regulars, who prefer soap operas to music videos. Monique's role within the tavern is to uphold the normative standards of social interaction, and her challenge to Tray is a reminder that music videos that are targeted at the young have no place within the tavern.

While Monique and the regulars rarely experience discord concerning the programs to be viewed, there is occasional conflict between patrons. This conflict occurs when the tavern is occupied by only a few patrons. At such times, patron-patron conflict is brief, and resolved by one patron telling another, "You got to play something for everybody." To which the patterned response is "I hear ya." The lack of serious conflict between patrons results in part from their general attitude toward television. Regulars perceive television as less significant than the face-to-face talk they can have with their buddies. Conversation has the greatest importance, while television is the background for conversation. Those who cannot live with these normative standards for viewing television ultimately move on to other social settings.

Patrons' Use of Television Content

Patrons, like other viewers, redefine television, using their own definitions to understand what they view.[4] Specifically, patrons use television in the following three ways: they personalize themes from television as a way of giving television relevance; they develop an imaginary relationship with television personalities that facilitates shared group interaction; and they challenge and evaluate media information as a way of reflecting on their own moral positions.

MAKING IT PERSONAL

Over the time I spent in the tavern, one of the first things I learned about television and tavern social life is that patrons actively personalize television themes. That is, they discuss ideas, topics, objects, or characters from television, while emphasizing their own thoughts, feelings, and attitudes. One regular or the group of regulars relates the television theme to "real-world" personal experiences. By doing this, patrons give the general ideas, topics, objects, or characters from television programs specific social meaning for life in Trena's. This reconstruction of TV themes is both an implicit and an explicit process. As individuals personalize themes, they create familiarity among the regulars by recalling and sharing their personal experiences, thereby providing intimate information about themselves. For instance, sex and intimacy are the staples of the soap operas, talk shows, and tabloids that make up daytime programming, and patrons often look to the television to help make sense of their own experiences in those areas.

As she watched television, Monique explained to Moe that the women on the television program made their money as phone sex operators. I added, "You know like 1 900 S-E-X-M-E." We laughed. As we were joking around, Charles Perez, the talk show host, had one of the ladies do a mock phone sex conversation.

Moe twisted his face to convey irritation and said, "See. Only those people that call there wanna hear that kind of stuff."

I said, "Yeah. It takes a certain kind of person to call those hot-lines."

Moe added, "I had a man or somebody that would call me at one o'clock in the morning. He called for about a month straight. He would call and breathe in the phone, and that was it. One night he called me, and I said to him, 'I been waiting on you to call so I can get my nuts off.' He hung up the phone on me and ain't called since. See, I think he used to get his nuts off by calling me up and intimidating me. As soon as I confronted him, he stopped calling me."

"How you know it was a he?" Monique asked.

"Well, I don't know what it was," Moe said, "He, she. I'm just saying he stopped calling after I confronted him."

Moe's response to the television program and the subsequent discussion about the anonymous caller provides the other patrons with intimate information about Moe. For instance, Moe expressed a sense of disdain toward people who use the telephone for anonymous calls, especially male callers who call males. Moe's disdain is consistent with the general attitude of the patrons, who through interaction demonstrate that Trena's is a place where men assert their masculinity and (hetero)sexuality. Following these beliefs, patrons' conversations about sex usually include the discussion of their direct experiences with individuals of the opposite sex. In the following interaction, the patrons discuss the theme of "one-night stands," which they personalize from the *Charles Perez Show,* a talk show that enjoyed some success in the mid-1990s.

As I relaxed in my chair, the Charles Perez *program returned from a commercial. Charles Perez said, "We have a specialist here who says that we should not expect too much from a one-night stand." Charles Perez then turned to a White woman who looked to be in her thirties. She had a short haircut and simple facial features that gave her a rather plain look. Perez said, "What do men want from a one-night stand?"*

David, a patron who was looking up at the television screen, said, "How does she know? She ain't no man." We laughed. The specialist continued explaining that men look for sex, passion, and excitement in a one-night stand. Then a woman from the program audience commented that women want the same things as men. The specialist responded, "Well, there are some women that may want that."

At this point, the patrons began discussing their own one-night stands. Monique joined in to share a story. She said, "I used to have this neighbor who lived above me, and she would have men leaping out the window, at least two a week. I would be in the back washing dishes, and I would hear the window upstairs open and see a man running down the fire escape. I would say, 'Whoops, here come another one.'" We laughed.

David and the other conversants moved the discussion of one-night stands from the level of what one should expect of one-night stands to what risks one takes in having them. Charles, one of the older male patrons, shared his personal experience.

Charles told of an incident in which he had gone to visit a single woman with whom he had established a sexual relationship. On this particular visit, he was sitting in the living room, and the woman was in the kitchen. As he sat watching television, a man opened the front door with a key, walked into the living room, and said hello to Charles, and then turned the television station. Charles completed his story, saying, "I immediately got my coat and hat and left the woman's crib. I didn't want to be involved in any argument that her and her boyfriend might wanna have 'cause I was there."

In telling his story, Charles also demonstrates his ability to share stories, like other patrons, in group interaction. He exhibits his social skills, while, at the same time, sharing intimate information about himself. Charles went on to suggest that his departure from the woman's apartment was a smart move that gave him the opportunity to participate in other transient sexual activities. For Charles, television provided the context for entry into group interaction and an opportunity for him to boast of his skills at navigating heterosexual relationships.

Talk shows and soap operas are not limited to exploring the "deviant" sexual behavior of adults but also introduce questions concerning the sexual behavior of adolescents. Patrons use such topics to reflect upon their own adolescent behavior. In the following discussion, David and Michael exchange criticisms concerning the promiscuity of a woman on the *Jenny Jones* talk show, while other patrons share their own early experiences with sex.

The Jenny Jones *show came on. The program was about promiscuous young girls who had been sexually active since the age of eleven. Some of Jenny Jones's guests were now thirteen, fourteen, and fifteen years old. Also sitting with the girls were their mothers. Throughout the program the mothers showed disgust at learning that their daughters had been having intercourse with a number of boys and men. At one point, a woman in the studio audience stood up and said to one of the thirteen-year-olds, "You got a real problem, sleeping around here with these boys. I got a six-year-old daughter, and if she ever came to me talking about sleeping with some boy, I would beat her butt." As the woman from the studio audience was talking, David, a patron, commented to the other patrons, "I bet that girl ain't but about twenty-two years old herself. When did she start having sex, sixteen?"*

The woman in the television audience continued, "I'm twenty-three years old, and my daughter would never do that."

Michael, who was sitting next to David at the bar, jumped up to tap David on the arm to congratulate him for his accurate guess of the woman's age. He said, "Look a there, you were right. She ain't but twenty-three herself."

David said, "See, I told you she wasn't that old." David and Michael began to count back her age and concluded that the woman had been seventeen years old when she became pregnant. Being more critical of the woman from the studio audience, David continued, "All she said was that she had a six-year-old daughter. We don't know if she got an eight-year-old son or not." He said this as if to suggest that the woman's first pregnancy actually could have occurred earlier than their calculated age of seventeen years old.

Steve, who had been listening intently to Michael, jumped into the conversation and exclaimed, "But hold on now. Some people get pregnant one time and grow from that."

Monique said, "Shit, I was fourteen when I got pregnant the first time."

Steve said, "Some people mature. I remember I was sixteen when I got my wife pregnant. She was only fourteen. My parents didn't play back then. You know parents didn't play. After my mother found out that I had gotten my wife pregnant, my mother said, 'Junior.' I said, 'Yes, Ma'am.' She said, 'You thought with your dick, and now you goin' live by your dick.' They took my little ass and signed me up in the army reserves at sixteen. Well, it wasn't the reserves then. They called it something else in 1948. They were paying seventy-five dollars a month. I would work in the army and get seventy-five dollars. I would have to send seventy dollars home to my wife. All I had was five dollars. It wasn't so bad, though, 'cause back then I could get me a pack of cigarettes with a quarter. I would have me some cigarettes and a little change left."

The patrons transformed the Jenny Jones topic of adolescent promiscuity among girls by discussing their own early childhood sexual behavior. Beyond the discussion specific to adolescent promiscuity, Steve also gives a sense of his life history that is not intentionally solicited by any of the other participants in this interchange. For example, Steve shares the fact that he served in the army in 1948, he smoked cigarettes (as he continues to do), and he lived with his parents, who were stern disciplinarians. All of this information was generated by the process of personalization in which Steve appropriated the talk show theme.

Like Steve, other regulars draw on the content of television programs to facilitate the development of familiarity, through personalization. Patrons make Trena's a familiar social space where they can relax and let down their guard—something they may rarely do in the "real" world—by reducing their uncertainty about others in the tavern. This means gathering information about the behavior, attitudes, beliefs, and identities of others. One way that the regulars get others to open up in conversation is by exchanging their own personal information as they discuss television themes. In doing this, the regulars create a sense of obligation among other individuals to share personal information. This leads to reciprocity, with each exchanging personal information and developing personal tavern identities.[5]

GETTING FRIENDLY WITH TV PERSONALITIES

Through frequent viewing, patrons come to perceive an interpersonal relationship between themselves and a television persona. This perceived interpersonal relationship—parasocial relationship—is an imaginary, one-sided friendship with the television character, especially soap opera characters.[6] Viewers learn the attitudes and behavior of soap opera characters and develop expectations linked to the characters' attributes. Knowledge of character attributes, story lines, and events in a character's screen life is an important resource for interaction among the patrons. Since patrons share knowledge of soap opera characters, these characters become incorporated as living personalities within the communal discourse of the tavern.

In their discussion of soap operas the patrons personalize their viewing experience by the tone of the discussion and by the gestures associated with that discussion. Their behavior suggests an intimate knowledge of, and an identification with, the characters. In some cases, this identification with the soap opera characters facilitates a discussion among patrons that takes on the tone and quality of a conversation about a "real" mutual friend. For example, Monique and Blonde, one of Monique's female associates who hangs at Trena's, discuss the soap opera *General Hospital*. Their awareness of the characters, settings, and plots is part of their social reality they share with others. The simple exchange between Monique and Blonde illustrates the significance that soap opera characters have in establishing a point of interaction between two individuals.

As we sat and watched television, Monique picked up the remote control and switched the television channel to General Hospital. *Blonde looked up at the television and saw a Black male actor on the screen. Blonde turned to Monique and asked, "So he back on here, huh?"*

"Yeah," responded Monique.

Blonde, with a look of shock on her face, said with concern, "What he doing in the hospital?" On the television screen, the actor was lying in bed and imagining a vision of his father standing by his bedside.

Monique said, "The men that killed his father tried to do the same thing to him." Monique sounded as if she were revealing her disapproval of the attempted murder of a close friend.

Monique and Blonde use their separately developed knowledge of the soap opera characters to interact with each other. The soap opera character becomes a social link between the two of them.[7]

Patrons, as they develop their parasocial relationships with television characters, come to share specific knowledge about those characters. This knowledge of characters helps patrons to interact with one another because they share the requisite information necessary to converse about particular soap opera programs. An important factor in developing parasocial relationships with television personae is the length of time a viewer has been viewing a program.[8] I witnessed many conversations like the one I describe next, in which patrons demonstrate the importance of extended viewing. Most of the regulars at Trena's have a long history of viewing soap operas and extensive knowledge of their characters.

Vicki, a soap opera character, was making noises as she was transforming into her split personality. She kept saying, "Not now. Not now."

Andre pointed to the soap opera character Vicki and said, "She still on here? She's been on here for thirty years."

"Yeah, and Erica Kane has been on All My Children *[another soap opera] for twenty-eight," Monique added.*

"I'm getting sick of Erica, too," Jason added.

"Look at Vicki, she's changing personalities," Blonde said, pointing to the television.

"She still does that?" I asked.

"Yeah," Monique responded. "She got a new split personality now, though. It's Gena."

"She's Gena now," Blonde confirmed.

Phillip looked up at the television and said, "Look at her." He paused and then looked around the tavern as if he were reflecting

*on the other male patrons' preoccupation with the soap opera. He
said, "You find now that a lot of guys watch the soaps."*

*Monique said in agreement, "Yeah, I know. I was watching one
day, and the phone rang and somebody said, 'Monique, are you
watching what so-and-so [referring to the soap opera character]
is doing?' I said, 'Yeah.' Then the person on the phone said,
'Watch this.' [A character on the soap opera had walked in on a
couple being intimate.] I said to the person on the phone, 'Who is
this?' and he said, 'Tony.' I said, 'Boy, what's wrong with you?' He
was watching the 'stories,' too."*

*Phillip added evidence to Monique's observation. "They got
soap opera updates on all the radio stations now. And most of
them are done by men."*

"Yeah, all of them are men except Melvin," Monique said.[9]

"Yeah. On WGCI. He is funny as hell," Phillip said.

"He is a sissy," Monique said.

"Monique, ain't he still a man?" I asked.

*Monique paused and then responded, "In some ways." We
laughed.*

Patrons' shared soap opera knowledge contributes to an in-
tergender exchange of ideas concerning programming created
by the television industry largely for female viewers.[10] In discussing soap operas, patrons share their personal beliefs or normative tavern ideas about a specific topic—in this case homosexuality. The introduction of topics concerning gender allows the
patrons to reaffirm notions of masculinity traditionally held by
working-class men.[11]

Just as patrons in Trena's develop greater intimacy with
one another through continued interaction, they also develop, through continued viewing, this same perceived intimacy with characters on television. Patrons come to have certain expectations of the characters. These expectations of soap

opera characters are reflected in tavern discussions. For instance, David implicitly calls into question the masculinity of one of the soap opera characters.

> *There was a scene on the soap opera where a female character was defended by Tadd, a male soap opera character. Tadd grabbed another male character and threatened him. As this scene faded to a commercial, David, a patron, commented sarcastically, "Oh, yeah, Tadd." David then turned to Monique and other patrons and said, "I ain't really seen Tadd have a good fight. He usually just throw one punch and it's over with."*
>
> *Monique contested David's statement. "Oh yes, he has. He got into a big fight."*
>
> *"With who?" David asked.*
>
> *Monique described the specific incident, which I could not follow because of my limited knowledge of the program.*
>
> *"Oh, yeah. That was a hell of a fight," David concluded.*

Parasocial relationships facilitate interaction between patrons because the patrons have a common point of reference. Entering the tavern with knowledge of soap opera characters provides patrons with yet another theme around which they can enter into conversation with one another and thereby increase the likelihood that personal information will be exchanged between patrons. The exchange of personal information does not occur in every interaction where patrons discuss soap opera characters; however, viewing of television and subsequent recognition of parasocial relationships remains an important impetus for interpersonal relations. Thus, patrons' parasocial relationships with soap opera characters and patrons' personalization of themes from soap operas facilitate the exchange of intimate information about themselves and the reaffirmation of the core values of their local culture.

EVALUATING CELEBRITIES

Patrons use themes from television to critically evaluate the lifestyles of celebrities. Unencumbered by the consequences of living a celebrity lifestyle, patrons freely convey their moral stance toward issues confronted by celebrities and implicitly elevate their own moral status by suggesting that the "high and mighty" world of celebrity life is rife with questionable behavior. Tavern conversation focused on the behavior of celebrities allows patrons to become familiar with one another's views concerning issues that extend beyond the walls of the tavern. Using their own implicit moral sense drawn from personal experience, patrons appropriate the lives of celebrities and reconstruct them in a way that is relevant to the social world of Trena's. For example, patrons discuss whether Mike Tyson, the often troubled former heavyweight boxing champion, should marry Latoya Jackson, an entertainer and sister of Michael Jackson, in response to a segment of the television program *Inside Edition*.

Tom and Shell sat near the television. After serving them their drinks, Monique looked up at the northeast television and saw a picture of Latoya Jackson dancing. Monique said to Tom and Shell, "They rioted over Latoya." Monique then walked down to the west television and turned the channel to the program Inside Edition. *The volume was up. The announcer was then telling the story of LaToya Jackson's refusal to strip during her performance at a strip club. At this point in the commentary, the camera flashed a scene of men fighting with the security of the strippers' lounge.*

"Look at that shit," Monique said disapprovingly. "And she supposed to be marrying Mike Tyson. They a lie. Mike Tyson ain't marrying her."

"I hope he ain't," Shell responded.

"They say she got a ring from him and everything. But Mike Tyson ain't marrying her. He got sense. He even fired Don King. . . . After he got out of jail, Mike Tyson fired Don King."

"That's good for him. You know he doing better if he fired Don King," Shell said.

The patrons' commentary concerning Mike Tyson and La-Toya Jackson amounts to celebrity gossip. Such gossip is important for helping the regulars establish their own "moral" identities.[12] Underlying the patrons' negative evaluation of LaToya Jackson is her public image as an outcast from the Jackson family. Mike Tyson, on the other hand, is praised as a changed man since he "fired Don King," the purportedly corrupt fight promoter, and looked to start his life anew. Tyson was further positively evaluated because of the implicit period of rehabilitation that he had undergone during his time in prison for the rape of a beauty pageant contestant, of which many patrons believed he was wrongly accused. To the patrons, marriage to Jackson would result in Tyson's fall from grace yet again. Patrons stake out moral positions in this interaction concerning celebrities' lives. They suggest that others—in this case Mike Tyson—should not live their lives with "corrupt promoters" or "women of ill repute."

Patrons' evaluation of celebrities is not limited to celebrities' imagined "backstage" performances but includes celebrities' "frontstage" performances.[13] With the proliferation of talk shows in the 1990s, the "frontstage" behavior of talk show hosts arguably has become one of the most scrutinized topics on television. The scrutiny with which individuals evaluate talk show hosts' "frontstage" behavior is evident in the following exchanges between Trena's patrons concerning Phil Donahue, a nationally syndicated talk show host. Phil Donahue is interviewing a women who had been the victim of an attempted murder by her husband.

"What is this about?" Blonde asked. As we explained to Blonde that the woman had been attacked by her husband, Phil Donahue announced, "We will return to this bizarre story in just a moment." The television program cut to a commercial.

"I can't stand Donahue. I hate Donahue," Blonde said.

"Why?" Lucas asked.

"Because he don't never let his audience get in the show. The Donahue show is about Donahue." She pointed to her chest and continued, "He keeps the focus on himself."

"Yeah. He don't let people get in," Lucas added.

"Donahue is just like that other guy. What's his name . . . Geraldo?" Carter asked.

"Yeah, just like Geraldo," Blonde responded.

"They like that, that, sensationalism. That's all they about," Carter said.

"Montel Williams is like that, too. He tries to be the focus of the show," Lucas said.

"But Montel let his audience talk. He lets the show go. Donahue don't," Blonde added.

For the regulars, talk shows should be audience oriented and not sensationalized—behavior that the patrons attribute to egotistical talk show hosts. Patrons' criticism of Phil Donahue—taken along with other contextual information about patron behavior—represents the patrons' expectation that focused group interaction should afford each individual the opportunity to communicate his or her position in a balanced flow of conversational give-and-take. It is this theme that the patrons communicated in implicit contrast to the behavior of Phil Donahue.

In the conversational atmosphere created at Trena's through patrons' personalization of television themes, patrons position themselves to evaluate the lifestyles of celebrities without having to confront the consequences of those evaluations. Being critical of a public figure's life does not involve confronting that individual; therefore, the possibility of counter argument from the object of criticism is removed. Patrons are the "judge and jury" of behavior and can elevate their status among their peers by claiming a moral position. This exchange of moral positions among patrons is important because it helps to sustain a sense of familiarity among patrons. Since patrons' criticisms are directed at individuals outside the immediate social setting, they do not threaten one another with moral judgments. Each successive cohort of "regulars" learns to share personal information by using an interactional style that includes the personalization of television themes, the development of parasocial relationships, and the evaluation of celebrity lifestyles as a way of sharing personal and intimate information, claiming identities, and building relationships.

Race and TV Talk

Unlike primetime television programs, soap operas, tabloid news programs, game shows, and music videos rarely give serious consideration to explicit discussions of race. Still, talk shows occasionally present explicit matters of race about which patrons can talk, but these programs are usually limited to discussions of interracial relationships. Given the programs' limits, the patrons' talk about race and television is also limited. Whereas patrons personalize general themes from television, they avoid personalizing racial themes from television.

For some patrons in Trena's, talk shows and, more generally, television provide them with a view of the lives of Whites. Patrons are given the opportunity to visit a world with which they may not be intimately familiar, even though they may interact with Whites on a regular basis in an institutional context, such as work or school. Since patrons sample "White life" through the eyes of media as a means of understanding Whites more intimately, they come to rely greatly on media representations of Whites and other racial and ethnic groups as a source of information. This use of television by African Americans for information about the "other" is similar to the way in which some Whites develop their conceptions of African American males through mass media.[14]

The reliance on media representations of the "other" is problematic because of the "fairy tale" nature of television. For example, it is not always apparent to the patron, let alone many other viewers, whether what they are viewing on television is an accurate depiction of Whites' lives. Patrons must therefore determine the extent to which television is making true statements about the lives of Whites. Some patrons are discerning and implicitly recognize the "hyped" nature of television.

> *Monique grabbed the remote control, turned from the video of the Beastie Boys (whose members are White and play an interesting mixture of heavy metal overlaid with rap lyrics) singing "Sabotage" and said, "Oh, no. I'd rather watch the stories." Louise agreed with her.*
>
> *Monique began switching the channels. She stopped at Channel 7, whose picture was fuzzy and sound distorted. Monique said, "OOpa. We can't watch no stories on that channel." She then turned the channel to the* Sally Jesse Raphael Show, *a talk show that featured two White females and a White male arguing about a wedding. Under the picture on the screen, the caption read, "Sister tries to stop marriage." Monique set down the remote control and said, "Let's watch the White folks tell lies about their lives."*
>
> *"Yeah, girl, you know they be lying up something on here," said Louise.*

Patrons look to television to provide information about Whites, although they recognize the inaccuracy of talk show depictions. The regulars' reliance on talk shows and other media is related to the fact that many have limited interaction with Whites, and thus the "White world" is made immediately accessible through mass media (even though some African Americans have limited interaction with Whites, they are more likely to have interpersonal contact with Whites than are Whites with Blacks).[15] This suggests that television, in fact, has an influence on the ways in which individuals develop conceptions of the "other," despite the individual's recognition that information provided by television can be inaccurate.

The regulars share a general belief that, because of race, African Americans and Whites handle similar issues and circumstances in different ways. For example, Bobby and Richard make observations concerning the differences between Whites and Blacks with regard to how White women and Black women respond to the same set of circumstances in male-female relationships.

For the second half of the show, Jenny Jones *focused on a man who wanted to leave his wife of one year for his girlfriend of seven years. This was supposed to have been the case two weeks earlier, when the man was originally invited to the show. However, on this show,* Jenny Jones *discovered that the man now wanted to return to his wife and leave his girlfriend. The program then went to a commercial break, and Bobby and Richard began talking.*

"Watch this be some White folks," Bobby said.

"Yeah, 'cause if it was a Black lady, she woulda' left his ass a long time ago," Richard said.

"You're right. Black women don't play that shit too tough. You can't be shifting back and forth between two. Either you goin' have her or you goin' have the other, but you ain't goin' have both of them," Bobby said.

"You know it," Richard said, as they both laughed.

When the program returned from the commercial, there were two White women on the screen who had been involved in a relationship with the White man who now wanted to return to his wife. Bobby turned to Richard and Kyle and said, "Didn't I tell you that they would be White?" They broke into laughter.

Bobby's prediction concerning the race of the people involved in the relationship is based on both his assumptions about Whites' behavior and his firsthand experience of African Americans' behavior in relationships. The interchange suggests that there are "real" differences in the ways that Whites and Blacks deal with relationships. In viewing Whites on these programs, the patrons are given the opportunity to highlight what they perceive to be differences between Blacks and Whites.

Patrons' discussion of Whites' interactional differences is based on African Americans' deeply rooted awareness of their own interactional styles. Through intraracial interaction, African Americans come to recognize particular patterns of interactional styles that facilitate interaction between themselves and other African Americans. When television presents information that does not fit into an African American's expected pattern of interaction, then the Black viewer assumes that the behavior being discussed is that of some other racial or ethnic group. It is important to point out that these expected interactional styles are significantly influenced by the social environment in which one has intraracial interaction. That means that members of the Black middle class do not necessarily share the same interactional styles as African Americans from the working class. These styles of expected interaction may also vary across geographic boundaries so African Americans' interaction in the southern region of the United States may be different from that in the northern region of the country, or in urban environments and rural environments. Patrons' expectation of certain intrarace interactional styles suggests that African Americans develop their way of seeing themselves through personal experience, whereas television contributes less to Blacks' knowledge about themselves than to Blacks' knowledge of Whites. For instance, Monique, who lives and works in homogeneous social settings where she has little direct interaction with Whites, develops a conception of Whites through her comparison of Whites and Blacks and her recognition of African Americans' interactional styles.

The introduction of interracial relationships on television provides patrons with discussion material. Patrons evaluate interracial relationships, often seeking to determine why these relationships fail or succeed. Implicit in the discussion of the failure of an interracial relationship is the patrons' belief that race is central to the larger problems that individuals face in interracial relationships. For example, patrons consider the break up of "Vanity," an African American and a former rhythm and blues singer, and "Adam Ant," a White male and a former rock star.

> The television was on, and one station was showing an interview with Vanity that detailed her breakup with Adam Ant and her battle with a life-threatening disease.
>
> "She [Vanity] was with Adam Ant. The White boy," Tray said.
>
> "You mean Adam Ant, the one that sing 'Goody Two Shoes'?" I asked.
>
> "Yeah, that's the one," Monique answered.
>
> "Yeah, Adam Ant told her he didn't wanna be bother with seeing her any more. He moved all of his shit out and left," Tray said.
>
> "That's what she get for messing with a White boy," Monique joked, and we laughed.

Patrons attribute the problems between Vanity and Adam Ant to race, suggesting that Vanity would not have had the same problems if she had been dating an African American. It is as if the patrons imply that African American couples do not experience unhappiness and decide to end their relationships.

Interestingly, if Adam Ant were African American, the patrons would not then be able to explain his departure from the relationship in terms of race but would need to look beyond race to find something more telling. Patrons' reliance on race to explain relationship discord demonstrates how general experiences are sometimes framed exclusively by historical race group experience. This race group experience not only frames the ways in which the regulars see problems in interracial relationships but becomes a frame through which individuals evaluate the authenticity of other African Americans. For the purposes of the current discussion, race group introspection occurs when African Americans evaluate the behavior or actions of other African Americans in a candid manner. This evaluation may be of African American institutions or individuals and functions to draw distinctions between various subpopulations of African Americans. For example, Greg draws a distinction between being Black and being a "real brother" on how a Black male television talk show guest talks.

The Jenny Jones Show *had an interracial couple on the program. There was a Black male who had a White girlfriend. The White woman's ex-boyfriend, a White male, complained that Blacks and Whites shouldn't be together. At one point the Black man, who was heavy and wearing a black suit with a black tie and white shirt, made effeminate gestures and said to Jenny Jones, "He [the ex-boyfriend] calls her house asking why she is with that nigger."*

Greg, a patron, responded to the talk show guest's statement: "You know he ain't no real brother. How many Black folks you know that say nigger? We say niggah. See, when we sitting around watching the game we say niggah. He said 'nigger.' I bet them White folks like that."

Greg's behavior in drawing the distinction between the talk show guest and other working-class African Americans is consistent with what many African Americans do when they use language as a way to draw distinctions within their racially homogeneous social settings. Even though Greg highlights the negative use of the term "nigger" by Whites, he also points out that for some African Americans, namely the group of African Americans of which he is a member, the term "niggah" has a very different meaning from the use (and the pronunciation) of the word "nigger."

Race group introspection by patrons goes beyond examining the use of words to explore what African Americans consider to be the race's or Black individuals' strengths and weaknesses in a variety of situations. Patrons evaluate themselves and their race on the basis of popular issues. For instance, at issue is the talk show guest's inability to maintain a relationship with his ex-wife.

I recognized the program as the Jenny Jones Show *that featured a Black male whose ex-wife left him to date a White man, who was also present on the program. The Black man was explaining that he didn't think that the couple should be together because they were of different races. At this point, Greg turned to the television and said, "That motherfucka a punk. How he goin' get on TV and talk about that shit? He weak if he let his woman get away like that. She left him for that White man."*

As the television commercial aired, Spice, who was sitting across from Greg, said, "I can't believe him, man."

"Yeah," added Jerome, "how a Black man goin' have his woman taken from him by a White boy? He stupid for being on TV with that mess anyway. . . ."

As the program returned from the commercial break, the Black female talk show guest said, "I left him because he wasn't treating me right."

The White male talk show guest responded, "They have a saying, 'If you ain't happy with the person you with and one comes along that's giving you something that you want, then you should be with them.'"

As the studio audience erupted into shouts of insult, laughter, and applause, the Black talk show guest turned to his ex-wife and said, "You can get with anybody, but you shouldn't be wit' no White boy." The studio audience erupted again.

At this point, Greg, who had become increasingly frustrated with the talk show guest, said, "Look at him. He just so weak. He shouldn't even be on the show. He can't represent a brother. Man, he just gettin' used up like that. That's weak. He is soooo weak."

For the patrons at Trena's, "a real man" should be able to keep his wife, despite advances by other men. More specifically, a "real" Black man should be able to fend off any challenges to his relationship, especially by a White suitor. Greg and Jerome take the African American talk show guest's inability to keep his wife not only as a poor reflection on himself but, more generally, as a representation to "the public" of Black men's inability to satisfy their wives. Underlying Greg's commentary are the stereotypes that have been historically offered concerning, first, African American males' physical prowess and, second, their sexual prowess. Greg's expectations of the Black male talk show guest are bound up in the historical conceptions of African American men as better physically and sexually endowed than their White counterparts. Accordingly, Greg suggests that, if historical conceptions of Black males are true, then the Black male talk show guest should not have lost his wife to a White male.

In addition to the patrons' explicit discussion of African

Americans' weaknesses, some patrons also implicitly highlight the strengths of Whites. The recognition of these strengths suggests that interracial relationships may be permissible if the individuals involved are being provided with something that they are not receiving from their intraracial relationships.

On the television screen was a White male in his twenties, who was built like a bodybuilder. He was sitting next to an attractive Black woman in her twenties, who was his girlfriend. They complained to Jenny Jones that they were being harassed by the Black woman's ex-boyfriend, who didn't want the White male and the Black female together because of the new boyfriend's race. When Monique saw the White male and Black female together on stage, she said, "She's cute. . . . And he's a hunk."

"You mean he's got a physique?" Vic asked.

"Hell, yeah . . . I don't care what they look like just as long as they can pick me up," Monique responded.

"Yeah," Vic added, "I done picked up a few in my days. My arms and legs done gone out on me, though." We laughed.

The program then introduced the Black male who had been "harassing the women and her boyfriend." The Black male was slender and not at all comparable in physical size to the White male. Vic said, "Oh, he look like he would do some scandalous shit. Messing around with other women and carrying on. That's why she left his ass alone."

Here the patrons employ a neutral stance toward interracial relationships, using "objective" factors such as physical appearance to measure the appropriateness of interracial relationships. Monique emphasizes the physical characteristics over racial characteristics, at least in discourse. Whether she would actually date a White male with a good physique is an entirely different issue.

Conclusion

Trena's patrons borrow from the general themes that television provides in order to elaborate personal experience. Since there are few programs during the patrons' viewing time that explicitly discuss race, the patrons have little opportunity to invoke their interracial experiences. Even when television programs focus on race explicitly, the programs are of a conflictual nature and limited to interracial relationships, relationships that patrons do not acknowledge having had. Given the specificity of television programs that deal with race and patrons' limited interracial experiences, patrons are rarely in a position to invoke personal experience in the discussion of mass media racial themes. This demonstrates one way in which patrons' life experiences have been limited to everyday homogeneous interactions with other African Americans, rather than convivial interactions with Whites. It is these unpleasant interactions with Whites that become the subject of serious discussion within the tavern.

Chapter Four

TALKING ABOUT RACE

I smacked the shit outta him 'cause he was over there at his bar calling our women bitches and niggahs. I don't care if they work for him. He gotta show some mother-fuckin' respect.

While growing up in the city of Chicago, in one of its many racially segregated neighborhoods,[1] I came to understand that racially segregated meeting places were sites where "niggahs" could be called "niggahs" and "whitey" could be called "whitey." Such settings have their roots in the historical relationship between Blacks and Whites. Prior to the civil rights movement in the United States, African Americans created racially homogeneous social settings in response to both de jure and de facto segregation. These spaces were seen as safe havens for African Americans to explore the meanings of race and other concerns that they could not or should not discuss in the presence of Whites. Today, however, many informal settings exist where amicable interaction can and does occur between Blacks and Whites. Despite the proliferation of interracial gathering places, racially homogeneous social settings like Trena's continue to be the norm.

Within the cozy, familiar, and racially distinct setting of Trena's, patrons talk openly about race, a potentially volatile topic in interracial settings. Both the content and the function of patrons' race talk is significant. The regulars' recollections of racial conflict, conspiracy theories, and race group inadequacy are attempts at giving meaning to race and coping with racial inequities and discrimination. Patrons' race talk raises awareness of racism and discrimination, forms the basis of race group self-criticism, and recreates individual self-image. By examining race talk, I look to expose how certain social arenas like Trena's contribute to African Americans' conceptualization of racial ideas.

Racial Conflict

Central to the patrons' racial identity is their understanding of the long-term racial conflict between Blacks and Whites. This conflict, rooted in the socially constructed ideas about race built up before and during slavery,[2] manifests itself both explicitly and implicitly in the patrons' everyday lives. Through their race talk, patrons demonstrate the complex and subtle ways that race penetrates their lives and helps them to formulate an African American identity. This identity is based on the notion among African Americans that they share a common history—one of victimization under slavery, racism, economic depression, and alienation.[3] The residual effects of this history continue to be reflected in contemporary intergroup relations between African Americans and other racial groups, especially Whites. The patrons' accounts of these experiences are telling.

CONFLICT IN THE PROFESSIONAL REALM

The regulars are of a generation of African Americans that has experienced economic and social success.[4] Its accomplishments as a group are due in part to social and economic opportunities created by a number of events, including White male workers' departure for combat in World War II, desegregation in schools and public accommodations, and the opening of racially restricted housing markets.[5] Although the regulars have "lived the good life," they remain aware of the historical racial tension between Blacks and Whites, a tension predicated on the notion that African Americans are biologically and intellectually inferior to Whites.[6] This notion of Black inferiority reverberates in the rhetoric over social issues such as affirmative action. For example, some argue that Blacks are unqualified to do certain jobs (e.g., manage large corporations) but are wrongly given preference to Whites through affirmative action programs.[7] Because of this underlying notion, Trena's regulars, like other African Americans, find that their ability as workers may be unreasonably questioned by White coworkers.[8] For instance, Hardy, a forty-year-old store manager for a retail chain, came to the tavern after work and discussed the challenges he faced from his White coworkers.

> *"I had to take some of them on this morning," Hardy said.*
> *"Say what?" Thomas replied as he turned to Hardy attentively.*
> *"Yeah. They think that Black folks don't know nothing about figures. I went to this meeting this morning, and they tried to tell me something and give me part of the figures. I straightened 'em out, though. Then I went to another meeting, and they tried to give me some more mixed-up figures. See, White folks don't think we know figures. When I started pointing these figures out, they were surprised."*

"Uh huh," Thomas said, nodding his head in agreement.

"See, they get they jobs 'cause they know somebody, not 'cause they know what they doing. I knew the figures. I felt good."

"Yeah, I know what you mean," added Thomas.

"They wanna question a Black man 'cause he the manager. If it was somebody White, they wouldn't try nothing like that," Hardy said. He took a deep breath, sipped his beer, and started watching television.

While his White coworkers' inaccurate presentations of financial statements were not a direct challenge to Hardy's ability, he read them as an implicit insult to his intelligence. He "knew" that his coworkers were challenging his ability as a manager on the basis of race. Some African Americans face difficulty in distinguishing between Whites' "honest" criticism of their work and those criticisms driven by racism. It is often easier for an African American to accept a professional challenge as an attack generated by race than to spend the time and energy necessary to uncover the true source of the questions raised about the individual's ability. If African Americans were to stop to systematically evaluate each challenge to their ability, their time would be consumed by investigations that would ultimately affect their work performance.

Interracial work settings are one place that the regulars come in contact with Whites as part of a professional relationship. Since Trena's regulars are middle class, they have the economic means to purchase goods and services that are provided beyond those in their neighborhood.[9] Because of these economic means, patrons may develop professional relationships with Whites outside the work place. The lawyer-client relationship is an example of the kinds of professional connections patrons develop with Whites. These relationships create the potential for African Americans to feel that they have received inequitable service from Whites on the basis of race. Carlton's experience is an example. Frustrated with his divorce settlement, Carlton discussed his White attorney's handling of his divorce case. Carlton received what he referred to as "some fucked-up service."

"Well, my lawyer sat right up there in court and damn near gave my ex-wife everything," Carlton said, sounding frustrated. "Shit, brothers just might as well represent themselves. When I told my friends how much my ex-wife was getting in the divorce settlement, they asked me, 'Was yo' lawyer with you?' Shit, I turned around and told my lawyer, 'My friends was wondering if you was with me when I went up before the judge.' It's like I didn't have any rights."

"You might have to report this lawyer dude to the American Bar Association," Webb replied.

"I got that number, too."

"Well, you need to call, 'cause you don't know what kind of rights they violating," Webb continued. "As a matter of fact, the new president of the American Bar Association is Black. They just got a new Black president. You should call him. Check him out so that next time you talk to your lawyer you can drop a name by him to see if he'll straighten up."

"Shit. I'll call up there and be like, 'Yo brother, my lawyer bullshittin' me—and he a White boy, too.' I'll tell that brother right away. You right. I should call him."

Patrons take solace in the fact that there are other African Americans in positions of power who have experienced negative encounters with Whites and are able to do something about those experiences. With this understanding, patrons are able to put closure on the previous day's situation and prepare to confront the next day's conflicts.

CONFLICT WITH THE POLICE

Although they are hard-working and law abiding citizens, the patrons have experienced numerous negative encounters with the police. These encounters derive for the most part from the commonly accepted presupposition by the police that Black males are "up to something."[10] The patrons tell narratives that focus on their encounters with White police officers, who, on the basis of scant evidence, have harassed them. For instance, I listened to Daryl, one of the younger patrons, recount an incident to Spice.

We had been watching television when a news story flashed on the screen about the arrest of a robbery suspect who was African American. Daryl said, "It's good they caught him, but did they have to stop all the brothers to catch him?"

"What do you mean?" Spice asked.

"You know what I mean," Daryl replied.

"Oh, yeah. They always stopping brothers," Spice responded.

"Man, last week I was coming from the grocery store," Daryl said, "and I turned onto to Fifty-eighth Street, and these two White officers pulled me over. When they got to the car, I asked them what I had done. One of them said, 'You kinda swerved funny back there when you made that turn. Let me see your license.' I gave him my license, and I didn't say anything because I knew what it was all about. I hadn't done shit, but they was pulling me over because I was Black. They ran a check on my license and then brought it back. They said, 'All right, you can go.' Shit, I was pissed. I know damn well White people swerve around corners and don't even get attention like I do. I hadn't even turned like that. It's like if you a Black man rolling, then you got to be up to something."

"You're right about that," Spice said. "I got too many stories to

begin to think about. They're all jumbled in my head as old as I am." We laughed.

For the patrons, their experiences with the police are a constant reminder that race does in fact matter, especially for those who have to deal with the inconvenience, humiliation, and anxiety of being stopped by police when they are doing no wrong. I found early on in my own tavern experience that sharing a personal story of police harassment helped me to build rapport with the patrons, many of whom themselves had suffered similar harassment. It was an opportunity for me to demonstrate to the patrons that I could identify with them as one African American male to others.

Hank had just come into the tavern and was complaining that two White police officers were following him. After a few blocks, they stopped following him.

I turned to Hank and said, "At least you didn't have to go through all the stuff you have to go through when you get stopped."

"At least not this time," Hank responded.

"Yeah. I remember me and my brother were driving along Fifty-fifth and King Drive. We had just made this left turn, and these detectives pulled us over. I guess they pulled us over because I was driving my mother's new car. Anyway, it was early evening and dark. They flashed the search light at the car and then told both of us to get out. They walked us around to the back of the car and told us to put our hands on the trunk. I said, 'What did we do?' The officer on my side shouted, 'Shut the fuck up. Where are you coming from?' I said, 'We just came from a friend's house, and now we're going home.' The officers started frisking us. After they finished one went to the driver's side of my mother's car and searched the car, while the other one stood

by the back of the car with us. After the one cop finished his search, he walked back to the back of the car and said, 'Y'all can go now. Just watch how you turn the corner.' When we got home, we told our mother and she went off. She was upset. She said, 'That is so damn humiliating. They stopping you in the street all out in public for nothing. Feeling all on your private parts and talking crazy. Then they don't even tell you why.' She was mad as all hell."

"See, man, that's the type of shit I hate," Hank said. "They don't even tell you why they stopped you. But of course you already know why. Because you're Black."

"Me and my brother didn't even trip 'cause it wasn't the first time," I said.

"Yeah, keep on living, and it won't be the last time, either," Hank said with a laugh.

These experiences are shared by the patrons and are grounded in feelings of alienation that have been created over the historical treatment of African Americans. As one patron asked rhetorically, "How can you feel safe when the people that's supposed to be protecting you always fuckin' with you for no reason?" This patron's comments are borne out by the recent reports that police officers in many U.S. cities use racial profiling—attributing criminal characteristics on the basis of a person's race—in their police work.[11] Thus, police, most often White, disproportionately monitor African Americans' activities. These reports only reinforce what Blacks have known all along: if you are African American, then police are inclined to stop you, detain you, or beat you without justification. Given these feelings, many African Americans view police as a threat to both their physical and their mental well-being, instead of as public servants and protectors. After all, it is difficult to shake from one's subconscious the image of police officers and police dogs attacking unarmed civil rights marchers when police harassment continues to be an everyday reality for African Americans.

PHYSICAL CONFLICT

Patrons tell stories that move beyond their mere frustration with their perceived inequitable treatment by police. They share narratives about managing their problematic racial encounters by resorting to an immediate means of defense, rather than reporting their problem to someone "higher up," as Carlton was encouraged to do concerning his lawyer. In telling these stories, patrons emphasize their successful negotiation of the negative racial encounter through physical means. For example, Jackson, a seventy-year-old patron, explains his immediate response to racial remarks made to him by a White customer in the restaurant where, as a young man, he waited tables.

> "I had nothing but four tables then, and after I finished with table number one, they had to wait if they needed something else once I got started on table number two. I didn't care if they wanted a glass of water, they had to wait. . . . So I was waiting tables, and this White boy said to me, 'Nigger, didn't I tell you to get me some coffee?' I had a tray of food in my hand and set it on his table and told him, 'I'll be right back, sir.' I went into the back and got some coffee and then came back to his table and served him. I poured one pitcher of coffee over his head, and then I hit him upside the head with the other coffee pot." Jackson gestured hitting the White customer.
> "You burnt him, huh?" Alvin asked matter-of-factly.
> "I poured it right over his head." We laughed.

Jackson emphasizes a bold act of immediate physical retaliation not only as a means of individual triumph but as a means of identifying with the "Black experience" of living in "White America." For the patrons, Jackson's story embodies a real sense of resistance to being addressed in a way that was standard in Black-White social interaction during Jackson's youth. With the continued sharing of experiences such as Jackson's, patrons develop a cultural repertoire for dealing with everyday interracial interaction.[12]

One basic tenet of the regulars' interactional repertoire is the notion of "respect." Respect is the recognition by others of an individual's human essence. To be treated with respect is to be recognized as human even if one has different cultural and social ideals. According to one patron, "If people don't respect you, then you don't have anything." The regulars believe that having the respect of those around you is necessary for meaningful interaction to occur. Some patrons hold respect in such high esteem that disrespect by anyone, especially Whites, pushes the patrons to defend their principles with a physical response. Those taking action are not always the victim of the intended or unintended disrespect. For example, Pasta and Webb share a recollection about Antonio, an Italian bar manager, who makes disapproving remarks about African Americans.

"You know who I can't stand out there in Carroll [a suburb of Chicago]?" Pasta asked.
"Who?" Webb replied.
"What's that motherfucka's name? Anto, Anton . . ."
"Antonio," Webb interrupted.
"Yeah, I can't stand that motherfucka."
"You mean Antonio the Italian?"
"Yeah, that Italian motherfucka."
"I can't stand him, either," Webb affirmed. "Let me tell you something. I smacked the shit outta him 'cause he was over there at his bar calling our women bitches and niggahs. I don't

*care if they work for him. He gotta show some motherfuckin'
respect."*

*"Yeah. That's why I don't like him. He calls you all kinds of
shit just 'cause he hired you to work for him. I can't deal wit' a
man like that."*

"He got to show you some respect!"

Stories and recollections like those shared by Webb may be
embellishments of actual events and may have limited factual
bases. Despite the possibility that these stories may be "untrue"
or "unreal," it is important to recognize that, for the patrons,
these stories serve as a way to negotiate the meanings of racial
conflict they have had with Whites. These narratives are retell-
ings of resistance to the pains of racism. Retelling these stories
within Trena's empowers patrons in a way that they may not
have been empowered in the original encounter. Such verbal em-
powerment might also be referred to as "talking shit."[13]

"Talking shit" is a kind of boasting or verbal jousting between
patrons as they attempt to outperform each other. If there is a
narrative that clearly represents this kind of jousting and posturing, it is Triston's presentation regarding himself as the mur-
derer of a White soldier. While this may be Triston's way of joking or of exaggerating his conflict with Whites, his statements
should be understood within the context of frequent overt racist
acts against African Americans in the 1940s and 1950s.

*"Let me tell you—and I don't tell everybody this—I was in the
service. The Black division—they had two divisions, the Black and
the brown division and they were all Black. And there was this
White sergeant—from Alabama or some other little White back-
of-the-woods place. And we was cleaning the road, and he called
me all types of nigger. I told him not to call me a nigger. He called
me all types of names and then said, 'If I had you in my town, I*

would tie yo' ass to the back of a truck and drag you all through
the town, nigger.' I said to him, 'You wouldn't want me in your
town, 'cause I would make you kiss my ass all through the town
square.' Then he put his hand on his gun at his side and, just as he
was about to pull it from the holster, I shot him. I shot his hand,
the handle off the gun, and an X through his chest. The army had
me charged with murder."

Robert, who had been listening intently to Triston's story, said,
"You had target practice on him. Shot him up, huh?" He then
asked cautiously, "Well, answer this for me. How did you get out
of it?"

"Well my sister worked for Dr. Yatzee and she told Dr. Yatzee,
and he got in touch with someone that knew the President. My
sister told Dr. Yatzee, who relayed the story to the President that
she had a brother that was about to be killed, but she wanted him
home. The President sent a radiogram, and I was in the barracks
going to the firing line the next morning, and before I knew it I
was on my way home. I had to spend nine years in jail for it, but
I'm here. And army investigators asked me, 'Did you mean to do
it?' I told them that I did. They asked, 'Why?' and I told 'em
'cause he was about to kill me. It wasn't no accident. Hell, naw.
See, I didn't bite my tongue."

Triston's narrative carries a cathartic relief, as if the events
had occurred yesterday. Both he and Robert ease the historical
pain of living in the 1940s, a time of great power imbalance between Whites and Blacks, by constructing and negotiating a
symbolic victory against racism; a victory not only for Triston
but for other African Americans.

Triston recalls this story prior to the 1998 murder of James
Byrd Jr., an African American who was beaten in Jasper, Texas,
by three White men, then tied to the back of a truck and dragged
until his skin was raw, several of his bones broken, and his head

severed.[14] This highly publicized case raises patrons' awareness of racial violence against Blacks by giving them a real life event that they confirm through mass media. Such events work to give enhanced validity to stories like Triston's and serve as constant reminders to African Americans that they remain vulnerable to violent attacks motivated by racial hatred. Patrons convey feelings of vulnerability through conspiracy theories.

Conspiracy Theories

Many Americans use conspiracy theories to explain crisis events or situations. They attribute these events or situations to the purposeful and clandestine actions of outsiders.[15] The mass media have recognized the appeal of these theories to Americans. Popular movies like *JFK* and *Enemy of the State* explore the deliberate and secret actions of Big Brother, for example, assassinating the U.S. president or controlling the American people through universal surveillance.[16] While conspiracy theories are used broadly, they are especially prevalent among those groups that have endured malicious assaults by outsiders in the past.[17] For example, African Americans used conspiracy theories during the era of slavery in America to explain their perception of threat to the African body.[18] These theories became a standard prism through which African Americans could view their position as victims of racially motivated attacks.[19] Today, cases of government abuse against African Americans have become further proof of Whites' ability to conspire against Blacks.[20]

For the patrons, constant news reports of employment discrimination, racially motivated attacks against Blacks, and police harassment help give explanatory power to conspiracy theories. Thus, within the tavern context, regulars invoke conspiracy theories to explain unusual events or situations. The familiar setting of the tavern allows patrons to offer, support, or reject conspiracy theories with little restraint. Some situations or events provide greater opportunity for creating conspiracy theories than others. One such event, much in the news during my time at Trena's, was the O. J. Simpson murder trial (O. J. Simpson, an African American Hall of Fame football player, was accused of murdering his wife and her acquaintance, both White. He was acquitted amid great controversy.). In the discussion I present here, Neecie, a bartender, shares her feelings about the trial. She offers various theories to support O. J. Simpson's innocence.

> I sat watching the O. J. trial on television. Neecie served Terrence and his friend their drinks. As she leaned over the bar toward them, she began gesturing with her hand for emphasis and said, "The Mafia did it. You know O. J. didn't do it. They ain't goin' never find out, either, 'cause if the Mafia want you to find out, you will, but if they don't, you won't. You know how I know O. J. didn't do it?"
>
> "Why is that?" Terrence asked.
>
> "'Cause look at the way they was killed. With a knife. That's how White people kill each other. Now you know that don't no Black person kill with a knife. We use guns. Especially the projects where O. J. from. Look at what they did to Michael Jackson and Michael Jordan. You know O. J. was set up. He didn't do it."
>
> "Yeah, I can see that," Terrence said.

Patrons build their conspiracy theories, like Neecie's concerning the O. J. Simpson trial, from their understanding of, first, urban violence among African Americans and, second, various public conceptions of the Mafia and other clandestine organizations. Urban violence among African Americans is often presented as random acts of violence that include gang drive-by shootings, carjackings involving the use of handguns, and street-level drug warfare. Such media presentations of urban violence suggest to viewers that guns are the weapons of choice among African Americans. Implicit is the notion that there are cultural and racial differences in styles of murders specific to Whites, Blacks, and others. Additionally, conspiracy theories that imply foul play by the police take on greater significance for the patrons because many have been the victim of constant police harassment. The fact that Mark Fuhrman, the primary police investigator in the O. J. Simpson trial, was White and had been identified as a racist by some only raised more questions among African Americans regarding O. J. Simpson's culpability. In such cases, conspiracy theories prove a reasonable explanation for the otherwise irrational occurrence.

As in Neecie's story, Trena's patrons also build their conspiracy theories by drawing from the presentation of the Mafia in movies like *The Godfather*.[21] In these movies the Mafia is depicted as a unified force, primarily involved in organized crimes and murder, with intricate political and social networks that extend throughout America. Some regulars, like many other Americans, believe that the Mafia is one of a few organizations sophisticated enough to pull off a murder, frame someone else, and then maintain the secrecy of the setup. The belief that there are a variety of organizations in America capable of such secrecy leave some African Americans feeling conspired against regularly. Again, actual events help the regulars, like other African Americans, believe in the validity of such conspiracies.

Celebrities like Michael Jackson and Michael Jordan are the subject of many conspiracy theories. For example, patrons provide conspiracy theories as explanations for the pop artist Michael Jackson's alleged sexual assault on a young boy who had been visiting him at his estate.[22] One popular conspiracy theory recalled at Trena's around the Michael Jackson "news" suggests that a father sent his young son to visit Michael Jackson so that the father could later accuse the pop star of sexually assaulting the son. This accusation of sexual abuse, according to the regulars' theory, was asserted by the father in an effort to pressure Michael Jackson for money to finance a movie. The patrons view the Michael Jackson incident as an attempt by a White man to destroy a prominent African American entertainer by making him "look bad."

Another conspiracy theory among the patrons purports to explain the murder of James Jordan, the father of the famed ex-NBA basketball player Michael Jordan. As the theory goes, the Mafia murdered James Jordan to get Michael Jordan to pay his large gambling debt. The Mafia then set up two small-time criminals who were later convicted of the murder. Both the Michael Jackson and the Michael Jordan conspiracy theories carried weight in Trena's and could be heard in other African American informal gathering places.

Although patrons believe that African Americans are conspired against, they occasionally offer evidence to contradict conspiracy theories. For example, in the case of O. J. Simpson, Alvin shares an alternative to the often-recited argument that O. J. Simpson was being framed.

"But you gotta remember O. J. had beaten up on his wife. Shit, he was married to a Black lady first, and she was gettin' beat up and she got out before it got too late. I believe O. J. was the type that said, 'Do what I say do,' and if you didn't he would just grab the woman. It's a lotta guys out here like that. They spend all they money on women, have them in nice cars, and then the women wanna say, 'huh?' when their husbands tell them what to do. The husbands get mad and say, 'Whatchu say? I put all my money into you, and you out here acting like you wanna act. Bitch, I'll kill you.'"

Despite such challenges to conspiracy theories, these theories continue to carry currency at Trena's. African Americans support these theories because it sometimes comes out that a group or individual has in fact acted to harm African Americans. For example, Susan Smith's implication of a Black male as the perpetrator of a carjacking and the subsequent murder of her two children reaffirmed African Americans' belief in ongoing conspiracies intended to hurt them.[23] Susan Smith had telephoned the police and purposely misinformed them that she had been carjacked by a Black male and her children kidnaped. Smith later admitted that she had murdered her children. However, by playing on the often-used media stereotype of Black males as criminal, Smith's report sent police stopping, searching, and questioning young Black males. While this search did not culminate in the conviction of a specific Black male, it did increase Trena's patrons' awareness that they, as African Americans, could be victimized by Whites. In the conversation presented here, Monique and Jeffery talk about Smith's original story.

"And that Smith lady had the police looking for a Black man, too," Monique said. "Talking 'bout he had a skull cap on and a plaid shirt. I said, 'Okay, Black man.' How he goin' be driving around town in South Carolina with two White kids in the back seat in a purple, orange, eh, a pink-ass car and not get caught?"

"They had a Black man on TV this morning. He said they stopped him looking to see if he was the one who took the kids," Jeffery added.

"Yeah, I saw that. What makes them think that a criminal would do something as stupid as that?" Monique said.

"Well, at least they ain't lock nobody up by mistake. All of this 'cause Susan Smith wanna blame a Black man. Everybody else was ready to jump on the bandwagon, too."

Perhaps the inconsistencies in Susan Smith's story would have been the basis for a conspiracy theory explaining how an innocent Black male had been charged with murder if Smith had waited until much later to admit murdering her children. Examples like the Smith case, no matter how infrequently they occur, compound African Americans' feelings of vulnerability. These occurrences become the basis upon which African Americans construct conspiracy theories to explain how Whites "are out to get Black folks." What is more interesting is those who believe in conspiracy theories are not necessarily the poor and uneducated African Americans—those often thought desperate to attribute their social problems to others—but tend to be individuals who have greater income, higher education, and more information about community issues.[24] This profile of believers suggests that middle-class African Americans, like Trena's regulars, develop a greater sense of vulnerability to conspiracies. Despite the regulars' recognition of conspiracy theories as viable explanations for some of the social maladies that African Americans experience, patrons also attribute Blacks' social problems to African Americans' own shortcomings.

Patrons' Race Group Introspection

One overarching theme thus far has been patrons' disapproving remarks regarding Whites. Regulars suggest that Whites are responsible for trying to harm African Americans or "hold Blacks back." While patrons attribute African Americans' social problems to the overt and covert efforts of Whites, they also criticize Blacks individually and collectively. Patrons are unlikely to make critical statements about other African Americans in interracial settings because of a tacit "us-versus-them" understanding among African Americans. This tacit understanding is grounded in African Americans' historical and present need to be united against Whites' racially motivated attacks. In the past, those Blacks who violated this normative standard by publicly scrutinizing other African Americans were ostracized as "sell-outs," "handkerchief heads," "Oreos," or "Uncle Toms." Today, African Americans' public self-criticism is more acceptable, yet remnants of the "us-versus-them" mentality remain. Thus, racially homogeneous places like Trena's continue to be important social spaces where African Americans can make critical self-assessments without fear of damaging what many perceive as the race's fragile social image in America.[25]

Race group introspection among patrons occurs when they candidly evaluate the behavior or actions of other African Americans. The regulars' evaluations involve general topics such as education, money, politics, or business; however, patrons highlight aspects of these issues by emphasizing problems thought to be inherent in African Americans. In evaluating others, patrons use terms that draw themselves to, or distinguish themselves from, the individual or institution under consideration. In the following example, Charles identifies himself with a group of African Americans that have endured slavery and other inequities. Yet Charles suggests that these historical problems no longer prevent African Americans from achieving. Blacks' problem of underachievement resides in their own mentality.

"If you look at Blacks, you could say that they have done well. Now when I say that, I mean looking at them in relation to other things, from a historical perspective. See, what? . . . slavery didn't end but some one hundred years ago. Going from a chain around your neck to where we are today in 130 years ain't bad. But we got problems. We still have the slave mentality. We haven't accepted the language or the education. We still rebelling. Shit, we could have been accepted the language. Let me tell you, we still

*got the same slave mentality. Where I used to work at, you could
see guys laughing at everything the White man say. He just
laughing. Now that's the slave mentality. Don't get me wrong, we
used to have to do that to protect ourselves. We had to bullshit the
White man so that he would think that we was happy and we
wouldn't get into trouble. But we still got that mentality and we
don't need it."*

Charles's affirmation of racial identity gives him license to
speak critically of African Americans as a racial group.[26] His
comments seem of little significance in a setting like Trena's, but
if he were, for example, a public figure, then his critical and
straightforward statements could be problematic. Given the political nature of racial issues in America, it is almost certain
Charles would come under attack by African Americans for purportedly damaging African Americans' image and supporting
racist views. At Trena's, the patrons recognize Charles's statements as his individual and honest evaluation of African American behavior, rather than see them as inflammatory statements
designed to further damage the already vulnerable image of African Americans.

Patrons occasionally reflect on the political positions of African Americans. They especially consider African Americans' inability to be successful in local politics. For example, patrons
discuss the 1995 mayoral elections in Chicago. The incumbent
mayor Richard Daley Jr., an Irish American and the son of former mayor Richard Daley, had just defeated Joe Gardner, a little-
known African American mayoral candidate, in the primary
elections. Roland Burris, another African American candidate,
was mounting what would eventually be an unsuccessful run for
mayor in the general election. The patrons discuss reasons why,
as an African American candidate, Roland Burris would be unable to defeat Daley.

I sat watching television with Calvin, Slick, Moe, Hawk, and Monique. Moe was talking to Hawk on the other side of the bar, and I heard Moe say, "And he can carry some White folks." I looked up to catch a little more of what Moe and Hawk had to say.

Calvin talked across the bar and joined the conversation. "What y'all talking 'bout, the election?"

"Yeah," Moe responded, "Roland Burris."

"Roland Burris ain't goin' win, and I'ma tell you why," said Calvin. "'Cause Black folks don't wanna get together. They have this fragment here and this fragment there, and they say to each other you can run and I'ma run. They don't wanna put the bullshit aside and back just one candidate."

"But Burris can carry some White votes," Moe responded.

"But not enough to win," Calvin said.

"Well, he don't need to carry a whole lot, if Black people get out and vote. They ain't goin' win with 40 percent voter turnout," Moe said.

"Well, they ain't goin' come out. See, we can't get them to turn out, so he ain't going to win," Calvin said.

"You know, I was sitting at home yesterday and watched for two hours right outside a polling place, and I only saw two people vote in the primary. Two people. Now that's a shame," Moe said.

Hawk, who had been listening intently, said, "Well, if Black people would get out there and vote, we could put whoever we wanted in office."

Calvin responded, "I'm with George Ryan. Was it George Ryan, Secretary of State, who said . . . ?"

Moe nodded his head in agreement and said, "Yeah, it was him."

"Well, I'm with him," continued Calvin. "We should have all young people register to vote when they have to go and get their drivers license renewed at eighteen. Some of these young guys out here need to get registered."

Calvin's disapproving comments are acceptable within Trena's, where there is a normative standard of sharing one's personal feelings even if these feelings express dissatisfaction with African Americans. Within the tavern there are no real consequences for voicing one's critical position toward African Americans; therefore, patrons spend time taking leave of the "real-world" constraints of being African American. This departure from racial status is one that they can maintain only in racially homogeneous social settings. In most other settings, African Americans are called upon to represent the voice of a unified racial group.

Given the constant racial adversities that African Americans face in the "White world," it is difficult for the patrons to accept the lack of support given them by Black institutions. For example, many African American communities are challenged by economic instability. Anchored by a few neighborhood businesses, these communities can suffer economic hardship at any time, even in middle-class communities like South Gate. It is troubling to the regulars that some of the small African American businesses receive little support from larger, more established African American businesses. Calvin and Slick consider the limited support provided to African Americans by a large Black-owned bank near South Gate.

"Black banks don't support our people," Calvin complained.

"You are right. Metropolis National Bank, one of the biggest Black banks in the country, only gave $1,000 to the United Negro College Fund. According to the bank, this was a large sum of money," Slick said. He continued, as he pointed to his Budweiser beer bottle, "I support Budweiser because they give a lot of money to the Black community. They gave five hundred thousand dollars to the United Negro College Fund when Metropolis Bank only gave a thousand dollars, and swore they were raising up hell giving that little change."

"One time," Calvin recounted, "I went to the Metropolis

*National Bank with one of their checks for seventeen dollars and
the teller told me that I would have to pay five dollars to cash
that check. I said, 'This is your check, and I gotta pay five dollars.
Fuck this, I'll take this to my damn bank.'"*

*Moe, sharing Slick and Calvins' displeasure with Metropolis,
said, "And if you go to Metropolis to get a loan, they act more
racist than anybody. They don't wanna give you a loan. They
worried we ain't goin' pay it back. If we can't get money from
them, who can we get it from?"*

Inside Trena's, patrons are able to make distinctions, take un-
popular political positions, and create individual self-identities
that evade the stereotypes heaped on them in their interracial
interactions outside Trena's.

As they compare Black and White institutions, some patrons
imply that Blacks are less competent than other racial and ethnic
groups. This is a very touchy subject outside the tavern, especially
given the ongoing criticisms of affirmative action. Still, questioning the competence of African Americans can become part of the
joke discourse at Trena's. Through comical statements, patrons
play up issues of competence they themselves address daily.

*As I sat sipping my soda, a group of patrons talked about cars.
One of the patrons suggested that there was a Black-owned car
manufacturing company. Josh responded, "What brothers you
know making cars? They ain't making cars. Who making cars?"*

"The Japanese," Ricky answered.

*"That's right. Ain't no brothers making cars," Josh responded
as we laughed.*

*"Well, they'll be making them soon. They'll be making them
over in South Africa," Hardy said.*

"Yeah. But four brothers under a hood ain't good," Josh joked.

*"Well, they already got a Black airline in South Africa, and it
takes you from D.C. to South Africa," Hardy replied.*

"What did you say?" Josh asked with a laugh.

"It takes you from D.C. to South Africa," Hardy answered.

"I thought you said it takes you from Chicago to D.C.," Josh said with a smile. "They can't take me from here to nowhere." We laughed.

"What's it called?" Ricky asked.

"US South Africa," Hardy answered.

"What they call it?" Josh quipped, "'Trust Us.'" We laughed.

"US Air trying to get them to change the name," Hardy added.

". . . Y'all know I'm just kidding. I think its good we tryin' to build up our own," Josh concluded.

Besides being part of Josh's exhibition of his witty social skills, his jokes play on the underlying theme of African American incompetence often suggested in interracial interaction.

Race group introspection becomes a part of how the patrons identify themselves as African Americans. Unlike their talk and action in the outside world, patrons can break from the group to be their "own man" and establish an individual identity that escapes the confines of the racial stereotypes held by larger society. In short, they can be recognized for their individual personality characteristics, rather than for their membership in a socially constructed racial group. Yet the patrons' stories, jokes, and questions regarding African Americans are grounded in the years of racial subordination that negatively impacted African Americans' self-conceptions. It is these subtleties of racism and discrimination that come through in the patrons' race group introspection.

Conclusion

Race talk is significant to Trena's patrons in at least three ways. First, patrons' stories of racism or discrimination heighten the other patrons' awareness of negative racial experiences. By sharing stories of racial conflict, patrons develop a collective memory of racism and discrimination that is broadened with each additional story told. Second, in retelling stories of racial conflict, patrons are able to reframe the events in such a way that they emerge victorious. They can relive a negative racial experience and enjoy the added twist of having triumphed even though this might not have actually been the case in the original encounter. Third, patrons are able to highlight the diversity of African Americans' views by making intragroup distinctions in their race group introspection. They can realize a self-identity that goes beyond race. This talk, occurring in racially homogeneous social settings, helps shape the way individuals think about race and the outside world, a notion taken up in greater depth in the concluding chapter.

Chapter Five

MARRIAGE, WOMEN, AND THE TAVERN

I ain't gonna let no bitch trick me outta nothing.

When I began my study of Trena's, I had been married less than a year. At that time I was unaware of how the men's stories and experiences would influence my own view of marriage and, more generally, male-female relationships. Today, I recognize that the patrons' talk highlights the fragility of relationships between men and women. I find most intriguing the extent to which the male patrons' discussions about women are dominated by talk of extramarital affairs, one-night stands, and the complexities of maintaining relationships with wives and girlfriends. Trena's patrons share a range of ideas about their relationships with women, but many of their ideas center on points of tension in male-female relationships. What these patrons have to say about their own relationships may provide one context for understanding the increase in divorce or separation and cohabitation among African Americans.[1]

The patrons view marriage as a noble ideal that marks the maturing of a man. As one patron stated, "It's good to be married and take care of your responsibilities." For the regulars, marriage is not the only means of showing one's commitment to a woman. Patrons also recognize "shackin'," or living with one's girlfriend without marriage, as a respectable relationship. Such cohabitation is thought to require the men and women involved to bear the same kind of responsibility as is borne by those in legally binding marriages; therefore, regulars often regard men who cohabitate as having marital status similar to that of men who are actually married. Hal, a married patron, commented, "If a man lives with his woman and his woman says he's gotta be home, then he just like any one of us that's married—he gotta have his ass at home." The regulars' notion of cohabitation as a viable form of commitment is consistent with the national trend toward more long-term cohabitation in place of marriage.[2] Like marriage, the sanctity of long-term cohabitation is challenged by the patrons' flirtations with infidelity.

Infidelity

While the men of Trena's view monogamous relationships as an ideal, they also recognize the reality and the frequency of extramarital affairs. These affairs are perceived by the patrons as essential to male-female relationships to the extent that the possibility of maintaining a marriage or a long-term relationship without sexual transgressions is less realistic than is the likelihood of remaining in a relationship in which the man does "mess around." In fact, many of the patrons construct their identity as men through their stories of infidelity, as Cody, a man married for twenty years, points out.

"I remember when I first got married," Cody said. "You know how it is?"

"No. What do you mean?" I asked.

"You always trying to be good, but I just saw too many women out there that I liked. You go to parties, and the women look good. You go to work, and they look good. You go to church, and they look good. You just wanna mess around. It's hard not to mess around."

"So you messed around on your wife once or twice?" I asked.

"Now you know I messed around more than once," Cody responded. "I had a few women early on. It was mostly because I had to get with somebody else. I didn't do nothing stupid though—like leaving my wife. I stuck it out in my marriage, and everything has worked out. But, boy, you know I had to cheat a little like we all do." He laughed.

"I guess I ain't got to that stage yet," I said with a smile.

For Cody, like many of the other patrons, talk about having a few extramarital affairs is everyday discourse. I initially had difficulty understanding why the men talked about extramarital affairs as commonplace. Hearing this talk was an intense education for me about the other side—the infidelity side—of marriage. The patrons were schooling me on the reality of cheating. As time passed, I learned that some individuals' talk of extramarital affairs was partly an attempt to elevate their own sexual status among their peers. Yet, underlying this exaggerated play at talk was an element of truth—these men do cheat on their women.

Though many of the patrons brag about their affairs, they also recognize that some of their peers do not engage in cheating. One faithful patron reasoned, "What you wanna mess up your thing at home for? Why would you leave a good thing for something else?" Still, those men who cheat, and those who do not, recognize extramarital affairs as acceptable behavior for men, but not for women. The patrons use a double standard in evaluating men's and women's infidelity. Their belief in such a standard comes through in their joking commentary about violence toward women who cheat.

> *We had been sitting watching television for a little while. Monique turned to the news. There was clamor among the patrons until a news segment came on the television about an explosion. Apparently, a women had parked her car in a Metra train lot and taken the train to work. When she returned to the train station, her car exploded. After the news announced the story, Rick, who was sitting at the far end of the bar, yelled, "Shit, I know what happened to her."*
>
> *"What you about to say now?" Terrence asked.*
>
> *"That car exploded 'cause her husband planted that bomb. He said, 'I'll show you about cheating on me, woman.'" We all laughed as he continued. "You know she was probably fucking around—and he was, too, but that don't matter—so he blew her shit up." We continued to laugh.*

Many of the men suggest that if they ever discovered that their wives were cheating, they would, "knock her out so fast" or "kill her." As David, a thirty-nine-year-old patron said, "I ain't even goin' mess with the man 'cause he don't know no better. I'd just kick my wife's ass." Patrons suggest that men are *predisposed* to infidelity and seek polygamous relationships out of "natural" desire, while women do not have this "uncontrollable desire." Why else would men take "huge" risks for a "little sex"? As Winton points out, some men are willing to take more risks than others, and these risks may prove fatal.

> *On the news there was a review of all of the murders related to domestic disputes that had occurred in courthouses in Chicago.*

Blonde, Monique's female friend, looked up at me and Winton and asked, "Y'all remember the man that shot his wife, her boyfriend, and hisself?"

"Naw," I answered. "When was this?"

"Not too long ago," Blonde replied. "The man came in on his wife at her apartment and she was in the bed screwing her lover, and he shot' em both."

"Shiiit," I said.

"I guess my man couldn't take it," Winton said.

"I don't know how he got in the apartment. I guess he had a key to his girlfriend's place," Blonde added.

"Can you imagine that? I would never get caught like that. I mean, how you goin' get caught in your own bed with your lover? They got too many hotels for that," Winton said emphatically.

"I'm hip. That is crazy," I said.

"I guess they were trying to save that money," Blonde said.

"So. That shit was stupid," Winton said.

"They saved twenty-five dollars, but they dead now," I said, as Blonde and Winton laughed.

Winton said, "And you know another women caught her man cheating and cut off his dick."

"I heard about that," Blonde replied.

"What? Again?" I asked, referring to the earlier news story about Lorena Bobbitt, who also severed her husband's penis.

"Yep," Winton said as he snapped his fingers. "Just like that. Every time I think about it, I start feeling it." Winton bent over on the stool and folded his hands across his midsection for protection. "They say he came home from drinking and messing around with another woman, raped his wife, and fell asleep. Apparently when he fell asleep his dick was hard, and she cut the motherfucker off and walked down the road and threw it in the woods." Both Winton and I began to squirm around on the stools as if we could feel the pain in our groin.

"Whatcha say?" Blonde asked as she laughed at the way Winton and I moved around on the stools. "Say it again," she added with a laugh.

Winton continued with the story "They found his dick and sewed it back on."

"I heard that he can't get an erection, though," added Blonde.

"Yeah," Winton replied. "But they say that the hardest part for him is the tube that they had to put in for his urine. They say he might be able to have an erection in a year or so. Now the chick is facing a possible twenty years in prison."

Stories like this one illustrate how the potential for death or dismemberment that faces those regulars who cheat is what enhances their reputation within the tavern. These men take risks, and those who live to tell about them are "real" men. The patrons who "mess around" acknowledge that balancing their long-term relationships and their recreational sexual affairs is difficult. In order for a patron to have status as a real man, not only must he cheat, but he must also maintain the secret of his infidelity from his wife and girlfriend. This proves to be a difficult task, especially since the secrecy of the patrons' affairs can be compromised by nosy friends.

Discretion and Nosy Friends

Patrons use discretion to ensure the secrecy of their affairs; however, most patrons also recognize that there is one thing that discretion cannot control—their wife's or girlfriend's nosy female friends. Terrence once described the type "You know the one. The kind of girl who is jealous that her friend has a good husband, so she's always trying to catch the husband doing something so she can run and tell the wife." These friends are the "tattletales" who concern the patrons. Monique's own story illustrates the point.

We had been talking about hanging around the tavern, flirting with the ladies, and messing around in general. Monique, always the conduit for talk in the tavern, began telling her own story. Monique began, "One night I was working down at Lou's Lounge, and this guy I was messing with. . . ."

"When?" I interrupted, shouting in a teasing, taunting voice. "It better not have been recently."

Monique smiled and said, "Why?" I didn't answer, so she continued. "Anyway, Rico came by Lou's Lounge to see me. He parked his Trans Am out front. You know it got all that custom shit on it, so you know his car when you see it. Well, anyway, one of Rico's wife's girlfriends was going to the store around the corner from Lou's Lounge and saw his car. So she calls his wife at home and tells her that Rico is in Lou's Lounge. That bitch [his wife] called up to Lou's Lounge. . . ."

Tim interrupted Monique and asked, "Did she know who you were when she called? Had she ever seen you?"

"Naw," Monique said.

"Then you all right then," Tim concluded.

Monique continued her story "Anyway, she called up in Lou's Lounge and wanted to speak to Rico."

Tim interrupted again "Did she go off on you?"

"Naw. She didn't even know who I was. She just went off on him 'cause he was at Lou's Lounge having a drink and her girl told on him. See, that's the kinda shit that fucks you up."

"You damn right," Tim said. "Nosy friends need to mind their own damn business, and everything would be just fine and everybody would be happy."

The patrons are always wary of jealous girlfriends who are willing to disclose the men's transgressions. The regulars' fears escalate when they discover that their wives' or girlfriends' female friends travel in the same social circles that they do. For example, Renee, one of the bartenders who worked briefly at

Trena's during my study, knew one of the patrons through his girlfriend. Since Renee had worked at the tavern only briefly, she had not developed the kind of rapport with the regulars that Monique had. This meant that Renee felt less loyalty to the patrons and more loyalty to her girlfriend, who happened to be dating one of the patrons.

Renee had just finished serving Sam a drink when Lance, a young man in his late twenties, came into the tavern. Renee remembered meeting him through one of her girlfriends but couldn't remember his name. She kept saying to herself, "What is his name?" Lance sat down and ordered his drink.

As Renee made Lance's drink, she looked up at the television. On television was a talk show about extramarital affairs. Renee began teasing Lance. She said, "Tracy is probably at home looking at that right now and don't know where you are."

Lance ignored her as if she might have him mixed up with someone else.

"You don't want me to call Tracy and tell her where you at, do you?" Renee said. Lance smiled. At this point I got up to use the pay phone. Renee served Lance his drink and walked through the opening in the bar. As she walked to the back, I could see her stop in the back room and pick up the telephone. When I finished at the pay phone, I went back to my seat and sat down. Renee returned to the bar a few minutes later. She called Lance by his name for the first time and said, "Lance, I called Tracy."

Lance was surprised that she knew his name. He asked, "Who told you my name?"

"You don't remember meeting me when you came over Tracy's house, do you?" Renee asked.

"Naw," Lance replied. As Lance sat trying to recall their prior meeting, Renee went to serve another customer. Lance looked across the bar at Jerome and made a face that conveyed concern. Jerome smiled at Lance and his predicament. I made a face and

thought to myself, "He should be careful where he hangs out if he is going to mess around 'cause he can get caught if he hangs out around the wrong people."

Although Lance was only having a drink in the tavern and not up to "no good," it was troubling to him that one of his girlfriend's friends could be working in his "spot." Fortunately for Lance, Renee did not last long at Trena's; otherwise he might have had to abandon the tavern as a hangout in order to put social distance between his home life and his leisure life. Other patrons are constantly concerned with putting social distance between their leisure lives and their home lives, especially when their leisure life involves sexual transgressions. Patrons spend time discussing a variety of strategies for avoiding having their transgressions discovered. These strategies range from getting a hotel on the other side of town to slipping in a "quickie" near the work site. Then there is the common misrepresentations that patrons make to others about their relationships with their lovers.

Bob had been sitting and talking to his lady friend for a little while. Most of us were watching television. Bob and his lady friend were several bar stools away from us. Bob was pretty low key as the rest of the guys talked. Eventually, Bob and his lady friend got the tab, paid Monique, and left. As they were leaving, most of the guys looked at Bob's girl. When the door closed behind them, Jerome said, "Damn."

"That's right," Tim added. "That girl is fine as all hell."

"Please, fellas," Monique said with a smile.

"Bob ain't doin' nothing with that," Jerome added. "He can't be hitting it."

"I bet he ain't," Tim said. "I know one thing. I like 'em like that."

"She got a big booty, too," Monique added.

Tim straightened his back in the chair so that he could get a better view of Bob's lady friend as they walked to the car. "I couldn't see because she got her shirt pulled down," Tim said.

"Bob say that's his cousin," Jerome said sarcastically.

Both Tim and Monique doubted her identity as his cousin. Monique said, "Yeah. When I'm messin' around, I tell everybody the man I'm wit' is my uncle."

"Yeah," Tim said. "And I make up something, too. Plus I don't like nobody to know where my spot is 'cause they get all up in your business. They'll come by your hangout and come inside if they see your car outside. That's why I go to the Best Western. It's right out there past the house." He held his hands about two inches apart and said, "They have drinks like this for only two fifty. And they have food. I sit right up there and drink and eat and talk shit to my lady. . . . Naw, I don't like nobody knowing where my spot is. And I sure don't want them knowing who my friend is, so I just make up something."

For the patrons, picking safe spots and trying to negotiate the identity of their lovers is an important part of maintaining their affairs. Monique, acting in her role as a regular (male) patron, comments not only about her strategy for introducing her lover to others but also on the fact that Bob's girlfriend has a "big booty." Even in "men's talk," Monique is able to settle into a role that opens the tavern up for free exchange about women. This allows her to take part in exchanges that would ordinarily be reserved only for men. She hears stories not only about how to get by when you cheat but also about how to make committed relationships work.

Making Marriage Work

Not all patrons view extramarital affairs and the manipulation of wives or girlfriends in marriages or long-term relationships as appropriate. Some believe that marriage is important and that effort should be expended by husbands to cultivate it so that it grows without the added tension that extramarital affairs bring. As one of the younger patrons in the tavern and one recently married, I discovered that a few of the older patrons were willing to take the time to school me on how to maintain my marriage, even though they themselves had struggled. For instance, Charles, who draws on his experience of being separated from his wife, offers me practical advice for making my marriage work even though he himself is still separated.

After Monique got done with her phone call, she came back into the bar area and started a discussion on good men. Monique said, "Good men are easy to find." Charles and I objected.

"Oh, yeah?" Charles said sarcastically.

"Oh, yes, they are hard to find," I declared.

"Naw," Monique said, "they ain't hard to find. You just gotta know where to look. All you guys ain't bad."

"I'm a good man, and my wife knows I am," I said.

"Well, if you a good man, that's good, because being married ain't easy," Charles said. "You can't keep up the lifestyle you had when you were single. You can't be hanging out running in the street and all that. When I got married, it took me four years before I started acting like I was married. It was four years before I started being married mentally. I had to make that change."

"Well, I ain't been married a year yet," I said.

"Aw, well, you ain't made the change yet," Charles said. "You gotta make the change. When I first got married, I didn't act like I was married. When you get married, all of the hanging gotta stop. I used to hang out with my friends. We used to hang out at the pool hall or the bowling alley. When I would go home to my wife, she would complain to me all night about how she was sitting up at home watching television and I wasn't there. I didn't start

acting married until I stopped hangin' wit' the niggahs I was hangin' wit' when I was single."

"Yeah. See, they could hang out and act a fool, but you really wasn't supposed to," I said in agreement.

"Right," Charles said. "I was the only one married, and when I got home my wife would complain. Her mouth would be this wide." He touched his finger tips together to make a huge O. "I would have to go home and hear that mess my wife had to say. Funny thing is, I could understand how she felt, too. Why should I be out in the pool hall with my friends while she at home? I wasn't doing nothing except wasting money. After a while I got me some married friends to hang out with. We met some married couples, and me and my wife would go to dinner and the other couples would go with us. . . ."

"I understand what you talking about," I said. "I used to go out all of the time, but now I don't go out that much. And if I'm going out I'll say to my wife, 'I'm going out to such and such a place, you wanna go wit' me?' She might say naw 'cause she don't like the place I'm going to, but then she'll tell me I can go ahead. I go on out, and then I come back at a decent hour."

Charles nodded his head and said, "Yeah that's right. Marriage is hard, too. You got to be in the right frame. You can't have your money and have her have her money. When you together, you have to go to the table with your wife. . . ."

"Yeah," I interrupted. "That's something we're learning about right now."

Charles continued, "You got to go to the table with her. Sit down and write it up and decide what you gonna pay and what you ain't goin' pay. You can't make it if you got separate money."

Beyond Charles's implications of infidelity committed while he was "hanging with his boys," he also identifies areas of conflict that become contested grounds among married couples. The lack of time spent with one's spouse and the different perspectives on how family money is to be spent frequently become the basis of conflict in marriages.[3] The light that patrons shed on such marital tensions has been useful for many of the younger patrons like myself. Charles's directives for helping me to maintain my marriage are also grounded in the patrons' beliefs that women have key responsibilities for making a marriage work. According to the patrons' way of thinking, the women's responsibility include "givin' it up," or having sex, "taking care of the kids," and "working somewhere to help out the family." Interestingly, the patrons expect their wives to make financial contributions to the household while maintaining their commitment to traditional female roles within the family.

Will hollered down from the far end of the bar to the middle of the bar where four patrons were gathered and asked, "Is that the free drink section?"

"Yeah. What's wrong with that?" Terrence responded as he laughed.

"I ain't worried about you, Terrence, 'cause I know you goin' spend some money if you sit down there," Will said.

As Will and Terrence discussed free drinks, Vic sat down next to Hank. Vic started complaining to Hank about his wife. "My wife keep talking crazy about money. So I finally told her yesterday, 'Look here, I wake up at 4:00 A.M. to drive that damn bus with niggahs breathing down my neck. I might as well quit busting my ass and let you take over if all you goin' do is lay there in the bed and complain about money.'"

"You right about that," Hank said with a laugh. "Ain't no need in me doing all the work and my woman stayin' at home and wanna spend all the damn money. It ain't right. They wanna fuss at you all day when they could be spending that time out there working."

*"That's right," Vic said. "She got to go out and work, too.
And she can't think just because she working she don't have to
take care of anything else. Don't nobody let me off just because
I work."*

Economic conditions have changed such that families have a
more difficult time sustaining a comfortable lifestyle on the sole
income of a working man.[4] Gone are the days when the things a
family needed could be bought on one income. The sweep of
technology, the increased availability of consumer goods, and increased consumption by families have created circumstances in
which it is more likely that both husband and wife will need to
work outside the home in order to sustain a family. Thus, patrons, like many other Americans who have witnessed these
changes, no longer view women as merely housewives but see
them as valuable workers who must help support the family. The
implied dual role of women—homemaker and breadwinner—
adds tension to relationships as women seek to free themselves
from domestic constraints and men, like the patrons, continue to
have expectations that women will fill both roles.

Courtship Games and Trust

As more women have joined the workforce, more of them have
claimed greater economic independence. They no longer have to
rely on men to take care of them or their children. Those economic strings that were once used to bind women to men have
lost a great deal of strength. This fact adds to the patrons' feelings that some women are out to get something "we got." Many
of the men take the position of Triston, who once said, "I ain't
gonna let no bitch trick me outta nothing." This attitude means
that some of the patrons see relationships as an opportunity to

enjoy sex, rather than to develop long-term relationships with women. When a patron does not follow this formula for successfully navigating male-female relationships, he is criticized by his patron buddies.

At one point, Spice and Sonny observed that Thompson was down on the far end of the bar talking to a lady, and Sonny said, "Look at Thompson."

"Look at him. All in her face," Spice added.

"You better keep an eye on him, 'cause you know he goin' spend all his money," Sonny said. "And I ain't loaning him shit."

"I ain't loaning him shit, either," Spice added.

"If he come down here," Sonny said, "and ask me for something, I'ma be like, 'What's up, Thompson, I ain't got no money.'" Sonny took a sip of his drink and then said, "That's a nice lil' lady he talking to, though."

Spice spoke to Sonny as if he were actually giving Thompson advice. "Yeah, but, man, don't be fallin' in love wit' em. Just hit it and keep on movin'."

"That's right, just stick and move," Sonny agreed.

"Don't be foolin' yo'self. They don't want no long-term relationship. They just wanna get what you got, too," Spice said.

Spice and Sonny had just finished talking about Thompson when Thompson came down to our end of the bar. As Thompson approached, Monique said, "What's happening, Thompson?"

"What's happening, Monique? What do I owe you?" Thompson responded.

"Seven fifty," Monique said.

Thompson sat down at the bar and leaned over toward Monique's ear and whispered something. Monique did not mention again how much money Thompson owed on his drinks. After a little more talk with the lady, Thompson left the tavern with her but didn't pay his tab.

Sonny and Spice view Thompson as a vulnerable man because he gives his lady friend too much attention. For them, Thompson's attachment will leave him with a broken heart because all his women really want is a part-time relationship and money. Accordingly, the men recognize brief sexual encounters as a normative aspiration for relationships. Since men and women understand the status of relationships, they all employ strategies to protect their interests when encountering the opposite sex. The men recognize this as they talk about strategies for dealing with women "looking for a freebie" on the first date.

> *"See, women be trippin'," Rick said.*
>
> *Frank, who was sitting next to Jerry and David, said, "I know. That's why I have my rule for taking women out for the first time. You ever took a woman out and spend two, three hundred dollars and you take her home and she talking about that good night?"*
>
> *"Yeah, man. I thought she would give me some kind of play," David said. "You know, a kiss or a little something else."*
>
> *"Shit, I can't stand that," Frank said.*
>
> *"That make you mad," David added. "It make you go back to your younger days when you would tell a girl, 'You goin' fuck, fight, or run.'" David and Frank slap hands in agreement.*
>
> *"That's why on the first date you take them out cheap," Frank said.*
>
> *"Yeah," Jerry added, "like McDonalds or some place like that."*
>
> *"Yeah. Or meet them in a public place or something. So they can't spend all of your money and then when you take them home be talking about good night. They need to give a brother a little ass or something. But they always wanna just spend your money. That's why I play 'em cheap on the first few dates."*
>
> *"I heard that," David responded. Frank and David laughed as they slap hands.*

David and Frank identify feelings that many of the men share. Although the patrons span a wide range of ages, most of them are disappointed with having to tirelessly play courtship games in order to get what they want. Similarly, the women these men court are also playing courtship games. The residual effect of such games is that men and women grow to distrust the intentions of each other with regard to the goals of a relationship. Oddly, the patrons recognize that their male peers especially fail to be trustworthy with regard to long-term relationships. I discovered these shared feelings during the early part of my research. During subsequent visits I observed that the patrons consistently reiterated their distrust for women and recognized men as unworthy of trust, especially in the matter of long engagements.

Monique walked over, and I ordered another beer. As Monique took my drink order, she noticed my left hand on the counter. She grabbed my hand, pointed to my wedding band, and asked, "What's this?"

"I'm married," I said.

"I didn't know you were married," She said.

As I reached in my back pocket for my wallet and pulled it out, I said, "Yeah. That's why, when you were talking all that shit about Rico in his Trans Am and messing around, I was like, 'You need to cool out since you supposed to be getting married yourself.'"

Sonny, who had been listening to us, turned to Monique and asked, "You married?"

"Naw," Monique answered.

I touched Monique's left ring finger as I said to Sonny, "She got some kinda ring on her finger, though."

"That's right, you suppose to be getting married soon," Sonny recalled.

"When?" I asked.

"We had to change the date," Monique said, "'cause he went to training in the police academy."

Sonny looked at Monique with a look of astonishment and asked, "You marrying a police officer?"

"Naw. My fiancé is a corrections officer. They just have their training at the police academy."

"So when y'all move the date to?" I asked.

"We didn't set another date," Monique responded.

"What? You didn't set another date?" Sonny said. "Now you know brothers are already scared about getting married. If you didn't set another date, then you know that's bad. All the guys I know like to keep women strung out. They keep telling them they're going to get married, but they change the date over and over again. My best friend Buck. He's really bad about that. He really strings them along and leaves them wondering, all the while he doing what he want to do. You gotta make your man set the date. Hmmm. So y'all didn't set another date?"

"Naw," Monique replied.

"You need to set a date," I said.

Monique turned to me and said in a sassy, sexy voice, "I ain't worried about it. He ain't goin' go nowhere. . . ."

We all laughed at her sexual innuendo.

The patrons fear that, without a long-term commitment, Monique is making a mistake. Underlying the patrons' feelings is the idea that the longer a man is uncommitted, the more likely it is that he will generate a multitude of excuses to avoid full commitment on his part. As so many patrons have said before, "Why buy the cow when you can get the milk for free?" or, why commit to marriage when you can have all the benefits, namely sexual benefits, without the commitment? The patrons, who themselves practice such manipulative techniques, are well aware that men create excuses to avoid marriage. Ultimately, the women they form relationships with are hurt by this lack of commitment. This very thing happened to Monique when she and her fiancé eventually broke off their engagement.

Perhaps the patrons' recognition of men's aversion to long-term relationships is the result of watching some of their married peers live a life under the control of their wives, or what they call being "henpecked." Those patrons who are thought to be under the control of their wives or girlfriends are the victims of teasing and innuendo.

We were talking about the Chicago Cubs as Oscar started for the door from the parking lot. I got up from my stool by the door and said to Monique, "He goin' want to come in."

As I unlocked the door, Monique said, "I guess his wife let him out again."

"Yeah she must have," Charles added. "His wife let old Henpecked out. Here comes Henpecked."

As I headed back to my seat Oscar entered the door. Monique didn't waste any time before beginning the verbal assault. She said, "Hey, how you doing? Your wife let you out again?"

"Hey, Henpecked," Charles added.

"Yeah she let me out again," Henpeck responded in a sarcastic voice.

"Yeah. How you pull that off?" Charles asked with a smile.

"See, I don't argue with my wife no more," Oscar explained. "I don't argue no more. She start hollering at me and saying, 'You shouldn't do that and don't do that no more,' all I do is reach into my pocket and give her a raise in her allowance and she quiet down. Then I can get out."

We laughed.

As the patrons weigh the constraints placed on their male peers' lives by marriage and consider the strains of courtship games, they often question the importance of long-term relationships. In fact, some patrons who have been in long-term relationships opt to terminate those relationships. Many times this termination is grounded in a patron's belief that he is being denied the freedom to do as he pleases, which is associated with being male.

Relationship Dissolution

Patrons often acknowledge that their girlfriends and wives can become truly demanding to the point of socially suffocating them. These men want to enjoy the freedoms accorded the successful single man; however, the social, sexual, and financial constraints that marriages or long-term relationships place on them prevent their enjoying these freedoms. These circumstances lead some men to dissolve their relationships. Sometimes these relationships are dissolved with very little conflict; other times there is a great deal of tension.

> *As we sat watching television, Green read the newspaper. Webb looked over at Green and asked him, "Man, are you all right?"*
>
> *"Naw, not really," Green replied. "I'm going through a divorce right now—and you know that song by Johnny Taylor, 'It's Cheaper to Keep Her.' Well, you better believe it's cheaper to keep her. Shit, if you go into court, then you might as well not go with a lawyer. Let me tell you, the lawyer just gone give it away. And the bitch be trying to take everything you got. . . ."*
>
> *"You shouldn't have that kind of attitude," Webb interrupted. "You should respect yo' woman. You loved her when you married her—if you say you didn't, then that's on you—so you should sit down with her. You tell her, 'I know we ain't getting along right now, but you know I love you. You can have anything you want*

that we have together and you can just give me what you think I should have.'"

"Shit," Green interrupted. "She goin' try to take all yo' shit."

"She can't do that," Webb countered. "Ain't no my shit or your shit. Y'all lived together. Can't no one person say that they have a right to all that y'all worked to build together. It's y'all shit."

Green took a sip of beer and mumbled, "Yeh well. . . ." then started reading the paper again.

Some patrons who have divorced their wives are hostile toward their former spouses because of their conflicts over material goods. Others have divorced simply because they "grew apart," and for these men and women, the divorce may have been amicable, as Hardy, now remarried, explained about his divorce from his first wife.

"I loved my first wife, but she couldn't keep up with me. I spent a lot of my time getting education, and she just couldn't hang. She grew spiritually, and I grew educationally, but her vision was too narrow. So we just decided to go our separate ways without any kind of negative feelings toward one another. We knew it just wouldn't work the way it was."

The basis for the patrons' peaceful divorces is a lack of conflict with their spouses regarding material goods. Such material effects come to represent the "booty" of a relationship that must be dealt with. These patrons do not dissolve their marriages at a young age. Normally those men who get divorced terminate these relationships after their children have reached adulthood and left home. As one divorced man pointed out, "I might have messed around on my wife, but as long as my kids were living with us, I wasn't moving out." To the patrons, it is important to maintain the marriage for the sake of the children, even when the adults no longer feel they should be together. This value of loyalty and commitment to the family seems to be fading among the younger members of the tavern scene.

Horace and I were discussing the marriage scene because he was thinking about getting married. We talked about the difficulties men might face when they stay with their wives after an act of infidelity. I said, "I don't know if I could leave my wife even if she messed around on me. I have a child on the way, and I think it's important for me to be around and for that child to be around their mother and father."

"Shit," Horace said. "I don't care how many kids I got. If my wife were to ever cheat on me, I ain't so sure I wouldn't kill her. I damn sure wouldn't stay with her. Ain't no amount of love for my kids going keep me in a relationship with her if I can't trust her."

"Well," I said, "maybe you're right about that trust thing, but I still think I would try to stay put."

"You know ain't nobody goin' live in a situation like that. Brothers coming up now don't have the patience for that. Especially since we don't have to worry about getting another girl. It's plenty for us around here."

For the up-and-coming patrons, the availability of other female prospects makes it easy to seriously consider leaving long-term relationships should questions of trust arise. The pool of marriageable men available to African American women seems to be shrinking. Everywhere the patrons turn, African American women complain about the low number of quality men. These complaints enhance the younger male patrons' feelings of worth. As the older patrons attempt to pass down values of relationship loyalty, they are confronted with the reality that young successful African American men are in short supply and in great demand among African American women. Thus, the younger patrons are less patient with relationships and are willing to "get out of a bad situation" by divorce more quickly than men who struggled with marriage in the past.

In addition to discussing their own experiences with divorce the patrons also examine celebrities' relationships. As suggested previously, patrons' use of information from mass media gives them an to opportunity to examine and critique the lives of celebrities as a way of reflecting on their own moral positions. Patrons can then pass judgment on celebrity behavior without passing moral judgments on one another. For example, patrons talk about Whoopi Goldberg, a comedian and actress, and her marital status.

"Did ya see on TV yesterday that Whoopi married a White guy?" Triston asked.

"She didn't marry a White guy," Spice replied. "He was a rich guy."

"What," I asked, "Whoopi got married?"

"Yeh," Triston replied. "You didn't know that. She married a White guy."

"That guy was rich," Spice reiterated.

"Well, Whoopi got her own money," Nelson added.

"Not like this man. He got money in his family," Spice said.

"Whoopi lost all her money, anyway," Triston said. "She married a Black guy first, and he took all her money."

"When she was married to the Black guy she didn't have no money. She had just come from the hood. . . ." Nelson said.

"You mean Harlem," Triston interrupted.

"Yeah," Nelson agreed, "Harlem. And she was still trying to make it. She was on the street. She was also a prostitute, so I know she wasn't just gone give up her money. That's probably why she fired them Black folks that worked for her. She wasn't about to let them mess over her money."

"Well, the Black man she was with before married her, and then when they broke up he got her money," Triston explained.

"She didn't have none," Spice said.

"What I'm saying is that he got all that she had," Triston argued.

"Well, shit. Two dollars ain't shit," I interrupted.

Nelson swiveled around on his stool and gave me a high five and said, "You damn right." We all laughed.

After we finished laughing, Triston picked up on the fact that Whoopi had married a White man. He said, "It doesn't matter if you or your mate is White or Black; if it's going to work, it's going to work. Shit, my wife said, 'If O. J. hadn't married that White woman, then none of this would have happened.' I asked my wife, 'Did you marry two men before you married me?' And she said, 'Yeah.' And then I asked her, 'What happened?' . . ."

Triston continued, "I told my wife, it ain't the color of the person. She always trying to say that the White woman is taking the Black man and doing something to him. Look, look. Look at Eartha Kitt, she married a White man; look at Lena Horne, she married a White man. And they doing fine."

Beyond the complexity that race and money can add to a celebrity marriage, the regulars also recognize that married people, more broadly, need some time apart. For the patrons, being apart means enjoying the good life by escaping the constraints of a relationship and spending leisure time with one's buddies.

A Man's Place

Patrons, through their talk, demonstrate that they lose patience with the male-female courtship games, the pressure of being accountable to their wives and families, and the struggles of work, all of which are exacerbated by racial conflict between Whites and Blacks. Given these constant strains on their lives, it is little wonder that the regulars feel they can escape the demands of their wives, family, employers, and society by relaxing in the tavern. Accordingly, the patrons work to ensure that the sanctity of the tavern is maintained, especially as far as eliminating the presence of women who might reaffirm their demands on the patrons.[5] Like other predominantly male gathering places, Trena's is maintained "for the men." As this interchange between the patrons demonstrates, those women familiar with the patrons recognize the boundaries that the men place to mark the tavern as their territory.

As we were sitting and drinking, a woman walked toward the tavern. As she walked up, Monique said, "Don't that look like Mary?"

"That's her sister, Carolyn," Moe answered.

Carolyn walked to the door and pulled it open and called to Moe, "Hey Moe, come out here."

Moe went outside the tavern. As the door shut behind him, I could hear Carolyn say to him, "I saw your car out here."

Moe talked to Carolyn for a few minutes, and then he came back inside. After Moe settled in his seat, Ben turned to Moe and asked him, "Wasn't that Andre's wife?" Andre is Moe's and Ben's mutual acquaintance.

"Yeah, but she getting a divorce from him," Moe answered.

"What was she looking for you for?" Ben asked.

"Naw, she wasn't really looking for me, but she said she saw my car, and so she decided to stop by and talk."

"Y'all not hooked up or nothing?"

"Naw. We used to date a while back before she and Andre got together. She said she saw my car, and she wanted to talk."

"Well, if you don't feel like talking, then you might wanna

hide your car. What I do is pull into the back of the building and then pull right up alongside of the building, and that way can't nobody see my car."

"Thanks, but I ain't too worried about the ladies coming in here to bother me. They know not to come in here when I'm with the fellas. That's why she didn't come in. She knows this is my spot."

Moe has already conveyed to those women he knows that the tavern is off limits to them. Carolyn's reluctance to enter the tavern is grounded in her recognition that the tavern is a man's place. Even if the men enjoy the company of their girlfriends or wives, they rarely invite those ladies into the tavern because their presence would alter the men's usually unrestrained talk.

Jerome had to go to work, so he finished his drink and told Monique, "Tell Thompson that I had to go to South Chicago."

As Jerome got up to leave, he saw Thompson pulling into the parking lot and said, "Never mind, I'll tell him myself." Jerome headed for the door but halted. As he looked out the window at a women crossing the street, he said to Monique, "I was about to go out there, but Thompson's lady is out there. Watch him. He's going to get a kiss."

Thompson parked his car and opened his car door. The heavyset woman crossed the street and walked up to Thompson's open car. Thompson kissed her on the lips. He then mumbled something. The heavyset women walked back across the street and on down. Thompson entered the tavern and had a seat by George.

George smiled as he said to Thompson, "How come your lady didn't stay with you?"

"I told her that she know that this my time to hang with the fellahs. So I sent her home. I promised her that I'd come by and give her some of that good lovin' later." George and Thompson laughed as they turned their attention to television.

The patrons are able to represent the tavern to their lady friends as a place for men to gather. To the spouses and girlfriends of the regulars, the tavern seems like a harmless gathering place for men to talk shit because other women are not present in the tavern to pose a threat to existing relationships. The women come to think of the tavern as a man's place in much the same way that the men think of the beauty salon as a place exclusively for women. It is a women's place to talk gossip and "chitchat."

There are women who frequent the tavern; however, these women have characteristically shared the interactional styles of the men in the tavern. They "cuss," "cut up," and "talk shit" on a par with the men. Yet their association with the tavern has more to do with the fact that they have an established friendship with Monique. Their presence, then, is taken by the men as part of the social atmosphere and not as a sexual opportunity to be pursued. Thus, their presence presents little threat to the patrons' relationships with their own women.

One might assume that, given the understanding that the male patrons establish with their lady friends regarding the tavern social space, that the sanctity of the tavern as a man's place goes unchallenged. Indeed, some of the patrons' wives or girlfriends do challenge the men in this regard. These challenges are met with swift responses by the men, who intend to maintain the integrity of the tavern.

We had been talking about hanging out in the tavern when Tim recalled a story. "Man, y'all remember Chuck, he used to come by here all the time."

"Yeah," Terrence responded.

Tim continued, "Boy, I remember that time he was sittin' in here one day, and his wife came looking for him. See, he had just got off work, and she was expecting him to come home so they could go out together, but that fool stopped off up in here to have a drink. He was sitting right over there." Tim pointed across the bar. "She came right in here and got him," Tim and Terrence laughed.

"What?" Terrence said. "Naw, she didn't come in here and drag him out."

"Yep," Tim said. "Now see. I'ma tell you. My wife only came to where I was one time. She came looking for me. She was with a friend of mine's wife, and they were together. So they were on their way here, and one of my partners had told me to meet him up at Duster's Lounge on seventy-ninth. So I went over there. I found out later that when she asked Nick, the bartender at Duster's, where I was, she turned to her girlfriend and said, 'Let's try to catch him at Trena's.' She didn't catch up with me, but then, when I got home I told her, 'Don't you ever come looking for me as long as you live. . . .'"

"I know that's right," Monique interrupted. "My fiancé don't come looking for me. He don't even come in when he picking me up from work. He just sit out there in the car and wait for me. I don't need nobody checking on me." We laughed.

"Now she knows not to come looking for me," Tim continued. "Especially when I'm in here with the fellahs."

Challenges by women to the exclusive male setting are dealt with immediately. Like Tim, the other patrons consider their time in the tavern "free" and see the tavern as "their's." Given their position on the tavern, some men do not even share the location of the tavern with their wives or girlfriends, in part because the men may be "up to no good" and, if their woman knew where to find them, they might be "caught."

Men Are Dogs

The tavern, as a man's place, creates a space where the men can easily talk about their sexual transgressions and how they treat women. As the patrons hang around and listen to the stories of others' "cheating," they become experts on the topic. They come to understand how men like themselves operate. For instance, regulars, like David, can accumulate practical information about male behavior, especially regarding how men treat women. Such information becomes useful when a man has daughters. Men can use this information to teach their daughters what to expect from men as they begin courtship. This knowledge comes through as David and Frank discuss issues of premarital sex.

"Did y'all see the Geraldo *show last night?" Frank asked. Nobody had. Frank continued, "Well, last night he had some eleven-year-old girls on there talking about having sex, and a couple of them were pregnant, too. That's a shame. . . ."*

David interrupted Frank "I got two daughters now. They sixteen and seventeen, and I couldn't go on no show with them talking about who they slept with."

"Not only couldn't I go on a talk show," Frank said. "I couldn't go in a counselor's office and listen to that. I'd be like, 'Okay, you did it once, don't do it again, and let's not talk about it anymore.'" He laughed.

"I'd be on the talk show stage and be up here. . . ." David swung his hand in an outstretched manner as if he were taking a swing at his daughter. "Swinging at them. I wouldn't even have to say a word, I would just swing. I'd say, 'You're my daughter, and your pussy is mine until you turn eighteen. Nobody else can have it. The fools out here ain't shit." He took a few more imaginary swings at the air.

"What daddies gotta do is to talk to their daughters," Frank said. "Take them out like the boys would and then talk to them so that they can understand what is going on. Let 'em know what's up with the boys. Tell them how the boys are dogs that just want to fuck around."

*David nodded his head in agreement and said, "You're right.
My oldest daughter, Aleece, got mad because my youngest daughter, Asenith had a boyfriend. I told Aleece, who went out and got a
boyfriend, 'Watch, Aleece, in about two or three weeks he goin'
ask you for some and you ain't goin' wanna give him none and
y'all goin' be broke up.' And, just like I told her, it happened. She
was upset for a while but wouldn't tell me why. Finally she told
me that the boy had asked her for sex. So I gotta agree witcha,
Frank, fathers do have to talk to their daughters to help them be
prepared for the stuff that the boys are going to be talking."*

David is as protective (perhaps overprotective to the point of
ownership) of his daughters as he is of his wife. Both David and
Frank suggest that daughters should be taught how men act and
how they should act in response to men's behavior. The contra-
diction is that David is teaching his daughters behavior—rejecting men's solicitations for sex even after the men have spent
money—that the patrons themselves dislike in women. With
such socialization by the sexes, the tension over the negotiated
body continues.

While the men are building negative attitudes toward women
who expect to be taken out and shown a good time before they
have sex, women are building negative attitudes toward men
who "act like dogs and want to screw around." Rarely do the
male and female perspectives on courtship come into conflict
within the tavern because it is a decidedly male social setting.
Occasionally, however, one of Monique's friends can challenge
the men within their social space. For example, Louise lays out
a verbal assault of her own against the men and their "dog"
behavior.

*We were listening to the jukebox. As the song ended, Monique
turned the jukebox down. Louise was sitting a few stools away*

*from me and close to JT. She overheard JT's conversation with
Thompson. They were talking about their sexual conquests of
women. Louise turned to JT and shouted in a joking manner, "I
don't wanna hear no old male chauvinist bullshit."*

*"Look here I been with the same woman for nine years," JT
responded. "I ain't cheated on her but once."*

*"Woof, woof," Louise responded as she turned to Monique and
placed her two forefingers above her head like dog ears. "Woof,
woof," she repeated. Louise then turned to my end of the bar and
said, "Look at all of y'all. Woof, woof. Damn dogs."*

*Monique made her way back down to my end of the bar, and I
said to her, "I ain't into it yet."*

"Huh?" Monique responded.

*"Old girl turned to me making dog sounds, and I told her that I
ain't into the doggie life yet and don't plan on it."*

*Monique smiled and took my money and walked to the cash
register. JT and Louise kept teasing each other. Monique walked
back with my change, and I showed her a picture of my daughter
in her basketball uniform. I said, "Look at this picture." Monique
took the picture and said, "Who is this?" I said, "That's my
daughter. The one I talked about in the newspaper."*

"Is that your daughter or your stepdaughter?" Monique asked.

"My stepdaughter . . . that's my daughter, fuck that," I reasoned.

*"I heard that," Monique said, "You takin' care of her so she is
yours. Just make sure you don't mess up your family by actin'
like a dog."*

*"You don't have to worry about that," I said as I stood up to
leave. Louise kept barking at JT, "Woof, woof. Damn dog."*

Both men and women have high expectations for marriage
and long-term relationships. Many of these expectations, at least
those that surface in patrons' talk, are rooted in traditional gender roles. Men expect faithful, submissive, and loving wives,

while women expect faithful, loving, and protective husbands. These expectations are challenged in reality since the regulars think it is okay to "hang with the fellahs," "drink and party," and "have a lil' honey on the side." This behavior by the regulars, and by men in general, creates and reaffirms distrust between men and women. Some women view men as "dogs" who are acting without sexual restraint. Many men, including the regulars, take pride in being labeled a "dog" and in having more than one sexual relationship. Still, these same regulars are quick to warn their daughters and sisters about the male "dog." As women guard against the "dog" and men guard against the woman "out for herself," both parties negotiate for an ideal relationship that is rarely reached. Perhaps it is this dissatisfaction that leads to high rates of divorce and separation among African American men and women, who lose out on the benefits of long-term relationships.[6]

The regulars, looking to escape the watchful eye of the women who so distrust them, turn to Trena's as a place of refuge. To ensure that Trena's remains a place to reaffirm their identity as men, the patrons admonish the women against visiting the tavern. The men adopt a number of strategies to exclude women from the tavern social scene, including use of deception and direct warnings to women against "looking for" their husbands and boyfriends in the tavern.

Such exclusionary practices are reminiscent of traditional male and female relationships, where women were made to stay at home while the men enjoyed interaction with other men.[7] Contemporary social and economic changes, however, have altered how men and women relate to each other. Women have fought for and achieved greater social equality and expect equitable treatment from men. Women have taken on more leadership roles in America's institutions and have gained a greater sense of independence. At the same time, economic changes have created opportunities for women to enter the labor force. Their active role in the labor market has allowed more women to become economically independent, although their pay lags behind what men receive for the same kind of work.[8] This combination of changes will be responsible for the redefinition of male and female relationships certain to be experienced by the next generation of regulars at Trena's.

Conclusion

The men of Trena's view marriage as a desirable goal. Having a family and developing a close-knit relationship with their wives is important to the men; yet some patrons compromise this ideal with acts of infidelity. Through stories of extramarital affairs and sexual transgressions, some patrons reaffirm the belief that male "cheating" is a "natural" part of many marriages and long-term relationships. Other patrons seldom share in this excitement about the breach of relationship trust; still, they too acknowledge sexual transgressions as commonplace byproducts of long-term relationships. When it comes to male-female relationships, most regulars believe in a "have your cake and eat it too" philosophy. Such a philosophy only adds to the already difficult task of maintaining a long-term relationship. Perhaps an appropriate description of the patrons' attitudes regarding relationships between men and women is that, while *much* has changed, *little* has changed. Nowhere is this stagnant growth of ideas concerning male and female relationships more evident than in men's talk about sex.

Chapter Six

SEX TALK AND INNUENDO

My lady is always at home waiting for me.

As a teenager, I would spend long nights with my friends hanging out and playing games of one-upmanship. Our talk was mostly about sex and centered on exaggerating our real, although limited, sexual experiences for the sake of fun. I find that Trena's patrons' talk around sex works in much the same way. The regulars' sex talk is more focused on fun and play than their other forms of topical talk. In sex talk the regulars are involved in a theatrical give-and-take, with each participant playing a part in the "performance" of jokes, innuendo, and stories about sex.[1] Much of what is shared in these discussions is expressed with the flow, timing, and rhythm of a tightly choreographed dance. Patrons make "cracks," "sound effects," and facial expressions on cue. While timing is emphasized as an important part of this form of interaction, the content of sex talk is rooted in the patrons' traditional notions of heterosexuality and masculinity. These underlying notions are the subject of this chapter.

Innuendo

Patrons implicitly and explicitly discuss a wide range of issues concerning sex. Their implicit talk takes the form of indirect statements or sexual innuendo exchanged through stories of everyday life. Within the tavern, the patrons sometimes transform seemingly unrelated stories into comical sexual innuendo. The regulars who are familiar with the tavern social scene are also adept at discerning implicit statements about sex.

William had not been to the tavern in a couple of weeks. He had been away in Jamaica for vacation. He had just entered the tavern to have a drink and talk about his trip. He took a seat at the bar and turned to Monique and said, "Give me some of that American whiskey. . . ."

"Okay," Monique responded.

"'Cause I don't want to see no mo' rum the rest of my life," William continued. "When I went to Jamaica them Jamaicans had rum everywhere. Rum and coke. Rum and coconut milk . . . and I don't want to see no mo' chicken, either. They had so much chicken until they jerked it." We all started laughing.

William explicitly referred to jerked chicken, a spicy seasoned Jamaican dish. To the patrons, the statement implicitly reminded many of them of "choking the chicken" or "jerking the chicken," both statements used among men to refer to masturbation. The regulars who are familiar with William and the tavern social setting come to expect innuendo of this sort. Implicit reference to sex is not exclusive to one patron but is shared among several patrons who join in on the fun. The regulars often demonstrate their tacit understanding of sexual innuendo through laughter or responses that further imply sex. Much of the implicit talk of sex has the manifest function of "talking shit," "teasing," or "having fun"; at the same time, these humorous approaches have the latent function of allowing patrons to address sensitive topics like masturbation.[2]

Antigay Sentiment

Beyond sexual innuendo, patrons also explicitly state their ideas about sex. As alluded to in the previous chapter, the patrons believe that a "real" man is a heterosexual man who practices promiscuity. Much of their talk is centered on reaffirming their belief in heterosexuality by telling stories of sexual conquests. Occasionally, a patron's heterosexuality is challenged through joke or innuendo. Such challenges are met with a rejection of homosexuality and a reaffirmation of the tavern normative standard that "men should be with women, not men."

County, who works at the county jail in Chicago, was describing to Shannon, Brian, and Ben how male inmates rape each other while they are in prison.

"Ain't nobody goin' fuck me . . . ," Shannon responded.

"You can talk all that shit, but you better not go to jail," County said.

"Ain't nobody goin' fuck me 'cause I ain't going to jail. Even if I did, I ain't gettin' fucked," Shannon said.

"You crazy. They got motherfuckas in there that's two hundred and fifty pounds and strong. If they wanna fuck you, they goin' fuck you," County said.

"I ain't gettin' fucked," Shannon said adamantly.

Ben, sharing Shannon's sentiment, added, "See, when they come up to you, you gotta knock all they goddamn teeth out so they don't fuck with you no more."

"Yeah, you have to," County conceded. "But the thing is, it ain't just one motherfucka that be coming up to you. It be about eight or nine. You ain't goin' fight all of them."

"I wouldn't get fucked," Shannon reiterated.

County shifts the conversation, implicating Shannon as the aggressor.

"Now tell me, if you were in prison and you got a murder sentence and you wasn't goin' get out, that you wouldn't fuck another man?" County asked.

"Hell, naw," Shannon said. "I tell you. There are only two things in this world. Life and women. If there are no more women, then fuck it, just kill me. I gotta have a woman. If it ain't no more women, then you gotta say fuck it."

"If you was in jail, you would fuck another man," County reasserted.

"No, I wouldn't," Shannon said as Ben laughed. "I understand what you trying to say, but I wouldn't. The only thing in this world more important than life is women. . . ."

"And money," Ben added.

"Yeah, and money," Shannon said. "A woman was made for a man."

"Well, if you was in jail, you would fuck. . . ." County started.

"I don't care what you say," Shannon interrupted. Shannon began gesturing with his hands for emphasis. "Let me tell you something. The last thing I can stand is a faggot. I don't care if they kill all of them . . . hol' up, hol' up. Tell me, who was in the Garden of Eden, anyway?" Shannon looked at Ben and Brian and paused.

Brian answered, "It was Adam and Eve, not Adam and Steve." We laughed.

*"That's right, it was Adam and Eve, not Adam and Steve,"
Shannon said.*

*Ben called to Moe across the bar and said, "Oh, Moe, guess
what he done said?"*

"What he say?" Moe responded.

*Shannon replied, "I said, in the Garden of Eden it was Adam
and Eve, a man and a women, not two men."*

*"You a damn lie," Moe said with a smile. "It was two sissies.
One of them just had titties on." We laughed.*

For the patrons, homosexuality is to be rejected outright and
heterosexuality is to be defended vehemently. Like many other
African Americans, the patrons disdain homosexuality because
they consider it stigmatized behavior that further weakens the
status of African Americans who already hold a tenuous social
position in America because of their race.[3] The patrons not only
reject the notion of homosexuality but reemphasize the sexual
importance of women. Accordingly, "real" men characteristically sleep with women and are willing to fight off a prison attack to preserve their "manhood" at all cost. Furthermore, patrons perceive homosexuality as a threat to the idea of manhood
within the tavern to such an extent that if there is suspicion regarding a particular patron's sexual identity, those who are familiar with that patron work to support a masculine and heterosexual identity for that individual. Such identity work takes
place especially during games of sex talk, when issues of sexuality become salient.

*Monique had stepped from behind the bar to go to the back
room. As she passed the opening in the bar, Rick playfully wrapped
his arm around her and whispered something flirtatious in her ear.
Monique didn't pull away but smiled and played right along with
Rick. Rick laughed and said, "You being nice to me today."*

"I got to show you I know how to act," Monique said. "The last

*time I did this to Al, though, he wouldn't leave me alone until I
cussed him out or something." Monique turned to William, who
was sitting next to Rick, and said, "William, you remember Al?
He used to come in here all the time. He didn't feel like I treated
him right until I cussed him out." They laughed.*

*"You talking about Al, the one that I thought was gay?"
William asked.*

*"Yeah. But, naw, he ain't gay. He comes in here from time to
time now with this chick on his arm," Monique said.*

*"Well, I thought he was gay because he used to dance like a lit-
tle punk. I saw him dancin' one day, and he was swinging his
arms like a little sissy. I call him the three sixes 'cause he got that
gay spirit in him," William said as he laughed.*

*Ted affirmed Monique's observations. "Al ain't gay. He be on
the women all the time. Every time I see him he talking to some
women trying to get her home."*

*"Well, I know when I let him hold me he wouldn't leave me
alone until I cussed him out. So I figure he can't be gay," Monique
concluded.*

In their play, both the patrons and the bartender challenge, re-
work, and reassert a masculine identity for one of their counterparts. In asserting the individual's tavern identity the patrons
are reaffirming Trena's as a place where men go to engage in
strictly male things. Although Al's masculine identity was challenged, there are few charges of homosexuality made within the
tavern because the patrons go to great lengths to present an aura
of masculinity when they enter the tavern.

Bedroom Performance

On the other side of the patrons' antigay sentiment is their belief that a measure of manhood is one's ability for high sexual

performance. Underlying this belief that sexual prowess makes a man is the notion that "a bigger dick is better," as one patron put it. Much of this thinking is rooted in the stereotype that African American men are more sexually endowed than their White counterparts. The historical images of physically superior Black slaves and the White women's supposed desire for "the big Black buck" reinforce notions of sexual superiority in African American men.[4] In fact, these images provide the basis on which many patrons joke with others within the tavern. Effective jokes cut to the core of manhood by implying flaccidity and a diminutive stature of the penis where patrons otherwise want to emphasize sexual endowment. From time to time, bartenders—especially during a day of "wide-open" sex talk—challenge this notion of endowment with jokes.

> *Monique had been talking to Hank at the far end of the bar. They were laughing and talking about sex. Monique came down from the far end of the bar and said to Cap, "Hey, Cap, check this out. Hank told me that this guy walked up to a lady and said, 'How can a big ass tell you if a woman got a big pussy?' The woman said, 'I got a big ass and a big pussy and all I need is a big dick to fill it, but you ain't got one." We broke out into a laugh as Monique added, "She told him, huh?!"*

Jokes about penis size bring a great deal of laughter within the tavern because these jokes play on the very stereotypes with which patrons are familiar. Notions of masculinity and heterosexuality are rooted in the traditional belief that real men "know how to do it," "ain't weak," and "can make the ladies scream all night long." The patrons' recognition of the significance of sexual performance to manhood means that many participants within the tavern social setting use sexual innuendo to transform everyday objects and events into phallic symbols.

Monique and Tina were both setting up for a special party that was to take place that evening at the tavern. Tina complained that she had to hurry and get set up so that she could go home and change clothes. Tina said, "I figured since it was my last week working here, I could at least put on my uniform."

Tina busied herself cutting lemons and limes and blowing up balloons, using a helium tank. After she finished the balloons, she began moving the helium tank to the back room by wobbling it side to side and inching it forward. As she wobbled the tank, Jerome asked, "You want me to help you move it?"

Maurice, who was also watching Tina, added, "Yeah, do you need some help?"

"Naw, I like this," Tina replied as she smiled and continued moving the tank.

The men watched Tina move the tank. Jerome finally turned to her and said, "I know why you like it. You like it 'cause it's big like something else you like holding onto." They all started laughing. I looked at the tank and noticed it was shaped like a large penis. I joined the laughter.

Tina played right along with Jerome's joke. She stopped moving the tank, rubbed her hand up and down the top of the tank, and said in a sexy voice, "I love its size. Oohh, it's big." We laughed. Tina then turned the valve on the tank and released helium. It made a short hissing sound. We kept right on laughing.

Monique joined in and said, "Tina, don't pay them no attention, they just mad 'cause theirs ain't that big." We continued to laugh.

The patrons rarely repeat standard jokes or lines from popular standup comedy routines; rather, they rely on their own stories of personal experience to convey their thoughts about sex. Some stories are involved and may reveal personal information that goes beyond what the average patron might expect to hear.

Still, it is through the sharing of their "private" sex-related sto-ries that patrons bring a realness to broad ideas about sex.

Winton turned and faced me, with his back to Blonde, and said, "I remember one time I had a knot on my testicles. Man, that shit hurt. One of my veins was clotted or something. You know that vein that runs up your testicles?"

"Yeah," I said.

"Well," Winton continued, "it got twisted, and the blood stopped moving through it. That shit brought me to my knees. I was in pain." Winton and I both started squirming in our seats. I could virtually feel the knot.

"Damn," I said, "how did you get it?"

"I just woke up one morning," Winton replied, "and got out of bed, and that shit hit me right after I stepped on the floor. I was rolling around on the floor trying to figure out what was going on. I got myself dressed, and I went to the doctor. When I got there and explained what I was feeling, the White boy said, 'You got T-something of the testicles. I forgot what he called it. Any-way, they laid me back and put two pads on the side of my balls and hit a switch. That shit felt better than an orgasm. It only took them two minutes to make that shit stop hurtin'." We laughed.

"Man, I know that shit must have been hurting," I said.

"I told that White boy that I would buy him a drink or some-thing 'cause he got rid of my pain. I thanked the hell outta him. Now I could get on with the business of tearing it up like I used to." We both laughed.

One assumption underlying the patrons' sex talk is that those who frequent the tavern are constantly in pursuit of their next sexual encounter. The patrons hold this normative expectation for both single and married men, although patrons recognize that married men have more restricted options. The regulars view the pursuit of sex as a necessary endeavor for a man, much like working a full-time job. Those men who live with their girl-friends or who are married are thought to have an advantage in the pursuit of sex. They are presumed to enjoy the opportunity for more sex because their wives or girlfriends can provide "in-house pussy." Some of the "less fortunate" single patrons use humorous commentary to transform the perceived advantage of having "in-house pussy" into a disadvantage.

While Monique was in the back room, Tyrone turned to Calvin and said, "I want some pussy. I got to find something to screw on the end of this dick."

Calvin, who lives with his girlfriend, bragged, "Now you know that ain't even no problem for me. My lady is always at home waiting for me."

"Is that why you can't go home to your woman?" Tyrone quipped. "Your girl done worn your ass out? She done drained you?" They both laughed.

"Naw, it ain't all that," Calvin replied.

"Then why can't you go home?" Tyrone continued. "'Cause you know if you go home, you gon' have to give her some."

"Naw, I ain't," Calvin said. "I ain't givin' her nothing."

"Shiiit. You will." Tyrone said. "She'll be like, 'Gimme some of that.' And you'll be like, 'Yes, ma'am.'" They both laughed.

"Naw, I won't," Calvin countered. "See, I know how to handle that. All I got to do is go in and start an argument, and that will take care of that. She just like any other women. She ain't gonna' wanna do it after that."

The patrons perceive that their power to control how much sex they have in a relationship is based on several factors, in-cluding whether they can "please" their woman. Some patrons talk about how long they make love as a measure of pleasing the women they are with sexually. Most patrons, however, recognize that talking about how long they can go in bed is little more than bragging as way of emphasizing the normative expectations of traditional masculinity. They also recognize the practical limits to daily sexual activity.

Monique, Charles, Hill, and I were talking about sex when Charles shifted the conversation to a discussion of good relationships. Charles said, "You got to be with a person with a good personality 'cause that sex don't last all the time." We all concurred.

"I hear that," Monique said. "Now the average man will have sex for, say, one hour every night. . . ."

Before she could finish, Hill interrupted her and said, "Shit, an hour. . . ."

"That's a long time," I said.

"I know that's right," Hill added. "Fifteen minutes is more like it." We all laughed.

Then Monique said, waving her hand, "Well, anyway. Y'all fuck for an hour, but it's twenty-three hours left in the day. So you gotta be able to get along with 'em when y'all ain't doin' it. Sex ain't everything. After the newness of the relationship wear off, you it's over."

"I know sex ain't everything," Hill said. "Me and my girlfriend only have sex once a month."

Monique erupted with laughter and said, "Shit. No, no, honey. We got to be fuckin' at least three or four times a week."

Hill tried to explain, "Well, I'm working two jobs, and we work very different schedules."

I pretended to be Hill talking to his girlfriend and joked, "'Okay, honey, on the thirty-first of this month, at X time, we will get together and have sex.'" We all started laughing. "That's rough," I added.

The patrons' notions of providing pleasure for their partners is not limited to the idea that "bigger is better" or that "you gotta last long and finish strong." There is also a recognition on the part of patrons that, beyond individual performance, there may be some social factors that affect how well men are able to perform sexually.

Patrons, in their discussion of sex, implicitly consider social problems that plague Americans. While the regulars may not make definitive statements about such social problems in their sex talk, the weight of these issues creeps into their games of fun and play. Their jokes about sex become a means to indirectly recognize, for example, how social problems like drugs bring difficult challenges to the next generation of "real" men.

The laughter died down as an attractive woman walked past the tavern. Rick saw her and stood up. He looked at us, put his hand to his lips, and gestured as if he were stretching his lips. He said, "Damn, she had some big lips. Them lips was out to here."

"She was with that young cat, though," William said. "But I'm sure she would get with me."

"Yeah, me, too," Rick said.

"You know what's wrong with these young cats?" William asked rhetorically. "They don't know how to eat pussy." William then pointed to Rick and nodded at me as he said, "You and that young fella goin' have to learn how to eat pussy to get set. The ladies like when you eat pussy." We laughed.

"I'm already set," Rick replied as he laughed. I just smiled.

Aaron overheard Rick's and William's comments and joined the conversation. He said, "It used to be a time when niggahs wouldn't dare admit to eatin' no pussy. Now y'all over here claiming it proudly. Boy, times sure have changed." We laughed.

"Yeah," William said, gesturing in my direction. "Well, maybe this young cat is already set." I sat on my stool laughing but

didn't say a word. William looked at me and continued, "You gotta know how to eat pussy to be set. That's why the ladies come to us, 'cause we know how to eat pussy."

"Shit," Aaron added. "Nowadays the young chicks don't come to us to eat them no more. They just come to get fucked since all these young dudes done got on that crack shit. They on so much of that damn crack that they can't even get they dicks hard. That's some fucked-up shit. How a man goin' be a man and he can't get his dick hard? That's why the ladies come to us to get what they need. We get all the women." We laughed.

The patrons imply that social ills like drugs are affecting the fulfillment of manhood. Being unable to effectively pursue women and have sex is a chink in the armor of masculinity. A patrons' male identity may be questioned if he is unable to "earn a decent living," "get the ladies," and "get down in bed."

Sexual Conquests

The regulars' emphasis on sex as a significant part of the male identity is readily seen in patrons' recollections of sexual conquests. These stories follow the pattern of a patron "macking," or "spitting game"—the art of enticing women for sex through talk—to the woman, taking her home or to the hotel, and having sex. Since the point of much of this kind of sex talk is to boast about one's ability, patrons participate in a game of verbal one-upmanship, with those listening to the stories often working to twist the ending in such a way that the storyteller loses face. These fun and games re-emphasize the significance of sex and heterosexuality for the patrons.

We sat watching television, although the volume was low. Spice and Terrence were starting to talk shit as Bo walked into the tavern. He exchanged pleasantries and then took a seat next to Spice. When Monique came over, Bo said, "Give me a cranberry juice. I haven't eaten anything, so I don't wanna start drinking."

"All right," Monique replied.

As Monique walked around the bar to get Bo's drink, Spice started telling Terrence and Bo another story of his sexual exploits. Spice said, "Let me tell you."

"Whatcha got?" Bo said with interest.

Spice continued, "I had met this women down at Lou's. We sat up there and talked for a little while, and once I get to mackin' you know they just can't resist. We were drinking, and I was feeling it. So, anyway, I took her to my apartment, and we did a little something. When I woke up the next morning, I was surprised as fuck to see her there in my bed. . . . But, anyway, when I first got her over to the house, we was kissin' and then I started sucking her titties. . . ."

"Is that all you sucked?" Terrence interrupted. We laughed.

"Be quiet, man, so I can finish my damn story," Spice said insistently. We quieted down, and Spice continued, "Anyway, I slept with her, and when I woke up the next morning I realized that I had made a big mistake 'cause she was still in my bed, she was ugly as I don't know what, and her pussy smelled something awful." We started laughing as Spice shook his head from side to side in disgust.

"Maybe that was your spit that made her shit smell like that," Bo said. We started laughing again.

The patrons take turns sharing stories of conquests and twisting the endings. Key to the patrons' ability to share in such sex talk is the bartender's position concerning the sexual issues that the regulars want to discuss. In order for the patrons to enjoy sex talk within the tavern, the bartender must be able to take a joke, enjoy flirting, and be able to talk about sex from a heterosexual perspective. Those bartenders who lack the ability to share in the tavern social life in this way normally do not last at Trena's.

Cuz and Monique were talking about some of the former bartenders who had worked at Trena's. They were tripping on Taneka, who worked for Trena's only a couple of days.

"She quit claiming she had to go back to school," Monique said. "But I just don't think she knew how hard it was to tend bar."

"Yeah, I remember her," Cuz said. "But she really only worked here for a few days."

"Yep," Monique answered. "That was it. She came in here, got trained, and then left. . . . What about Tess? Do you remember her?"

"Yeah. Wasn't she kinda short with long, pretty black hair and worked here a long time ago?" Cuz asked.

"Yeah, that's her. . . . I gotta tell you what was up with Tess, anyway."

Immediately after Monique made her comment about Tess, Cuz looked at her and then lifted his hand from the bar and shook it from side to side.

"You knew she went both ways?" Monique asked. "I didn't know she was a dyke until she stopped working here."

"Yeah, I knew she was," Cuz answered.

"Why didn't you let me know if you knew then?" Monique asked with a smile.

"Well, it ain't my job to go around telling you when they lesbians," Cuz replied. Monique and Cuz laughed. "The only reason I knew is 'cause I was in here talking shit and she wasn't really playing along, so I figured she wasn't on the up-and-up. It was the way she was kinda standoffish. She wasn't no fun, so I figured she didn't really like men."

"Well, I really didn't know," Monique responded. "Good thing she gone." They both laughed.

Heterosexuality is a strong theme among the patrons because it forms the basis for men's "macking"—flirtatious talk. To the regulars, macking to a lesbian bartender "just doesn't work."

The Bartender as Sexual Object

The female bartender plays a significant role in sex talk. She is the focus of much talk, and her ability to "play" the sexual foil for the men is a requisite for working at Trena's. Bartenders who have the ability to play along with the men using sexual innuendo, whispering voices, and hints of eroticism are enjoyed most by the patrons. Since the men are in the tavern to enjoy social life and to build their male identity, they want to be able to flirt with the bartender and be flirted with by her. This is evident in their comments to Monique, which range from passing innuendo to downright dirty talk.

I had been sitting for a little while sipping my drink and watching television. Monique had gone a few stools down to get Charles a drink. When she got to him, she asked, "Whatchu havin'?"

"I think I'm goin' have my Heineken on ice," Charles replied.

"I gotcha," Monique answered.

As Monique bent down to get Charles his beer, Charles peered at the cleavage in Monique's shirt, smiled, and said, "Monique, do you use silicone?" I smiled.

Monique hesitated as if she hadn't quite heard what he had said. She then realized that he had asked her whether she had used silicone to imply that her breasts were surgically enlarged. She raised up from the bar and propped her chest out and said, "Please, honey, are you crazy? That's an insult. These are all natural." We all laughed as she bent down to get the beer.

The patrons view Monique as an outstanding bartender. Her influence on the tavern social scene becomes apparent when patrons comment on other bartenders who serve as substitutes on the rare occasions Monique is absent from work. The patrons complain to one another that they "won't be able to have fun today 'cause Monique ain't here." Monique is quite adept at balancing her roles as the sometimes passive woman who needs attention, the aggressive flirt, and the tavern buddy. Her balance between raw sexuality and masculinity is interesting: one moment Monique is the object of explicit sexual language; the next moment she is sharing a story that parallels the men's stories in aggressive posturing and profanity.

Still, Monique's central role is as the object of fun and play, especially during sex talk. Even when the men are teasing and joking with one another, Monique is used as a prop that can be played off as men participate in a game of oneupmanship.

Monique knew what Jerome was drinking, so she poured his drink and left it near Thompson, George, and Slim. Jerome sat with his friends and drank and talked. After a few minutes, Jerome got up, walked to the opening in the bar, and called Monique over. When she came over, he leaned over and whispered something in her ear. She looked at him and then leaned over and whispered something in his ear. As she was whispering, Jerome looked down at Monique's legs.

George, who had been watching this whole interchange between Monique and Jerome, hollered, "You can't handle that. Ain't no amount of shit you talkin' gonna help you, either. You can't handle it." Thompson, George, and Slim started laughing. Jerome ignored the laughter and kept staring at Monique. The laughter continued. Finally, Jerome broke his stare, smiled, and walked back to where his friends were sitting. They just kept laughing at Jerome.

Being a passive participant in jokes or innuendo about sex is only part of how Monique handles sex talk in the tavern. Her role as the passive object of humor can be contrasted with her aggressive style of interaction during "wide-open" sex talk. Sex talk becomes "wide open" when a patron declares, "It's time to talk some shit" or "Y'all must be talkin' shit up in here." This is an announcement to all participants that they should expect tavern interactions during this time to be of a comical, theatrical, and witty nature. In this talk, Monique and the patrons dispense with sexual innuendo and move into more explicit talk about sex. This conversation style can last for a few minutes or for a few hours. Its duration is determined by the patrons' attentiveness to the "game." Their attention to explicit sex talk might be interrupted by television themes or by the introduction of more serious matters into the conversation. Even so, sex can remain the underlying theme, to be called on at any time during a regular's visit to the tavern. In some instances, Monique initiates explicit sex talk.

The tavern was busy because liquor deliveries were being made. Monique had taken the delivery man to the back to show him where to put the liquor. When they came from the back, the truck driver was talking to Monique, but I didn't quite hear what he said. As they neared the main bar area, Monique smiled and said in a low voice, "I can't help you with that, but I can sit something on your dick for you."

The delivery guy started laughing. He looked a little embarrassed. He said, "I know it's time for me to leave now. Y'all gettin' down and dirty."

"I told you we in here talkin' dirty," Monique said.

The truck driver folded his order forms and said in a challenging voice, "Y'all talk that sex shit, but who goin' do something?"

"Go on, Monique," Jerry said with encouragement. "Get him. He talking all that shit." We all started laughing.

The delivery guy smiled as he walked to the door and said, "Bye, y'all."

Sex talk can be embarrassing and offensive to those patrons who are not familiar with how the regulars and the bartenders behave. Like the liquor delivery man, many newcomers or first-time customers may be thrown off balance by the openness of talk within Trena's. Those patrons who are not offended by the regulars' sex talk—and other forms of talk one might consider offensive—continue to visit the tavern to become participants themselves. Such self-selection means that those who can enjoy a social atmosphere like that at Trena's become regular customers. It is rare that there are individuals present in the tavern who might be alienated by the regulars' conversations about sex.

On one of my first, visits Willie, one of the younger regulars, had been in the tavern for a few minutes showing Tina, the evening bartender, a bracelet. After he showed it to her, he left the tavern. When Willie left, Aaron turned to Tina and asked, "Why you think Willie keep coming back to let you try on that bracelet?"

"He wants me to pay for it," Tina said.

"Naw. What I think it really is, is that he likes you. That's all." Aaron said with a smile.

"Well, I don't know if he likes me or not. I just know I ain't got no money for a bracelet, but I do have a credit card." Tina and Aaron laughed.

"Shiiit," Aaron said. "You don't need the credit cards. You got the best American Express between your legs." Tina laughed as Aaron continued, "You don't even have to pay for the bracelet. Just charge it on your pussy." They laughed.

Tina looked over at me and noticed that I was smiling. She came over to me and put her hand on my hand and patted it and said, "See, this is what you goin' hear when you come in here."

"Y'all ain't bothering me none," I said.

"That's good, 'cause we talk dirty sometimes," she said as she walked back down to where Aaron was sitting.

Patrons and bartenders may be considerate of others; yet, this consideration for the sensibilities of others is limited to maintaining social civility and does not extend to an overall reframing of behavior to reduce the sex talk, which may sometimes be offensive to one or two patrons. Again, the patrons view the tavern as a home away from home and share the normative expectation that those who frequent the tavern will share in games of sexual innuendo. Some patrons even take the opportunity to share in sexual innuendo by telling stories about their "wildest sex fantasies." These stories are told with a humorous twist.

While we were talking and watching the Cubs game, Jerry came in and had a seat next to Snaggy. Jerry ordered his drink and lit a cigarette. As the television went to commercial break, Jerry started talking to Snaggy about some women he had met. Jerry said, "I met this bitch last week, and she asked me was I into the kinky stuff."

"Where?" Snaggy asked.

"I was wit' my boy when I met her downtown," Jerry answered. "Anyway, she asked me was I into the kinky stuff, and I said, 'Yeah. What kind of kinky stuff you into?' She said, 'You ever had anyone walk on your back with spikes on?' I said, 'Naw. But I could try it out.' She put on her shoes and started walking on my back, and I said, 'Ohh, ohh, this feels so good.' I told her, 'Now take your shoes off 'cause I ain't never had anybody walk on my back without shoes on.' She took off her shoes and started

walking on my back, and I said, 'Damn, baby, take them mother-
fucking spikes off.'" We started laughing as Jerry continued, "She
had some rough-ass feet. You know, the kind with the corn husk
up to her ankles." We all laughed.

The regulars share stories like this that amount to little more
than their effort to interact and enjoy the leisure time that they
have away from the outside world. Patrons can interact with one
another around a common theme—sex—with which most patrons have had some kind of experience. Sex as a topic serves as
a baseline subject for fun in much the same way that sex and violence are the baseline themes presented as television entertainment. It is one of the most common themes and has the widest
appeal to the greatest number of people.

Beyond understanding their sex talk as a way to enjoy tavern
life, patrons also recognize that the bartender's role as the sexual
object is limited to talk. The regulars do not expect that their sex
talk with Monique as the foil will lead to an actual sexual encounter between Monique and themselves. The patrons' understanding is due in part to Monique's ability to convey to the
patrons that sex talk "is just talk." For example, Monique elabo-
rates not only her feelings about sex talk but also her expectations of relationships beyond the tavern.

Monique, Hill, and I were talking about sex. Our conversation
started when Monique commented about Mary, a bartender who
works at the nearby Lou's Lounge. Monique said, "Mary gives sex
to just about anybody. They come in there talking the shit, and
she act like it's real. She be sleeping with the customers, and she'll
do it for cheap."
"Are you serious?" Hill asked.
"Yeah," Monique answered. "Y'all know I don't play that. Even
if I was meeting men at the tavern, they would have to treat me

right before we did something. You have to take me out more than once. And don't think 'cause you took me out and we had sex that you could mistreat me. Shit. You know how guys are?"

"Yeah," I answered. "They wanna treat you crazy after they get a little something."

"They like to act like they done something special 'cause they had sex," Monique said. "They talk about how they got that pussy." Monique pretended to talk to a man she just slept with and said, "Yeah, motherfucka, you got the pussy, but I still got it. See, I'll give you some at night, and the next morning I'ma still have pussy. Shit, I'ma have pussy until I die." We all started laughing.

The regulars recognize Monique's role as a bartender and a central reference of talk that is just talk. Monique is key to making the tavern a place for fun and play because she serves as the sexual foil for the men. Her age, attractiveness, and social ability make Monique an ideal person with whom the patrons can share the fun and games of sex talk.

Conclusion

Through their sex talk, the patrons implicitly and explicitly exchange their ideas about sex and sexuality. They assert their heterosexual ideals and their masculine identity through recollection and performance of their experiences. Within sex talk the male-female relationship is a key duality. Men are the aggressors who must have their sexual desires met, while women are thought of as objects to be pursued and conquered. In some cases, the patrons tell their stories of sexual conquest with an occasional twist that emphasizes a humorous aspect of sex or is an act of oneupmanship. The retelling of stories becomes a means by which the individuals in the tavern establish their social identity as good storytellers or "someone with something to say." Still, being a "real man" is also important to the patrons. They believe that real men are those who are able to perform well in bed and who have many sex partners. These beliefs are consistent with traditional beliefs about masculinity held by many Americans. The patrons' normative focus on traditional masculinity means that those who are not prepared to frequently engage issues of gender from a traditional masculine perspective are very unlikely to receive a warm welcome from the regular patrons at Trena's. Of course, there are occasionally violations of the general ideas about masculinity, but patrons are quickly guided back to the appropriate cultural position concerning such issues. Given the stability of the regular clientele at Trena's, there are very few challenges to this ideal. In fact, it is not unusual to see a "fresh face" one day and never see that face again, presumably because Trena's—with its emphasis on traditional masculinity—is not the place for this person. In this way, the stability of the clientele and the affirmation of traditional ideals is maintained. The social implication of such stability in tavern patrons is discussed in the final chapter.

Chapter Seven

THE PARADOX

If we fail . . . we are destined to drag the tradition of racial and ethnic conflict behind us, and drag this country down with it.

As a patron of Trena's, I have learned that the tavern serves as a local gathering place where patrons can safely claim positive identities for themselves. They exchange narratives about everyday topics, such as race, sex, work, and male-female relationships, thereby building individual and group identities. I also have learned, however, that a paradox exists in social gathering places of patrons, not only those of African Americans but in the informal gathering places frequented by people from a variety of racial, ethnic, and social class backgrounds. The paradox, stated simply, is that racially segregated gathering places facilitate the positive affirmation of racial identity, while compounding negative impressions of those outside one's racial or ethnic group. Study of such gatherings in socially homogeneous settings becomes relevant for understanding how individuals develop their outlooks on life and interact with others beyond the immediate social setting.

Trena's, like other informal gathering places, is a "third place," a public place "that hosts the regular, voluntary, informal, and happily anticipated gatherings of individuals beyond the realms of home and work."[1] Within the tavern, patrons converse with one another and maintain a sense of social tact. Each patron is given the opportunity to express his ideas, although these ideas are most often consistent with the normative standards of others who frequent the tavern. The patrons emphasize traditional notions of masculinity—dominance in male-female relationships and heterosexuality. The men also share racial identification—"the feeling of closeness to similar others in ideas, feelings and thoughts"[2]—with one another. They display this connectedness through disapproving talk about Whites, racism, and discrimination.

Identity and Catharsis

Negative talk, like that among patrons, about "the other" occurs in a variety of socially homogenous settings and is nothing new. For instance, in gender-homogeneous talk groups, women complain to one another about men, just as men complain about women; in segregated office talk, rank-and-file employees criticize management, just as management criticizes the rank-and-file; and in faculty gatherings professors gripe about students, while students in their informal talk gripe about professors. It is partly through sharing their negative experiences within segregated talk groups that individuals form or reaffirm a particular social identity, especially racial identity within urban settings.

One reason that urbanites emphasize racial identity is that much of America's urban population lives in racially segregated neighborhoods,[3] creating high levels of segregation within neighborhood institutions such as taverns, laundromats, barber shops, local restaurants, and coffee houses. These institutions continue to draw members of the community who share similar racial or ethnic backgrounds, values, norms, and beliefs. The neighborhood social gathering places are de facto exclusionary and create an environment where a regular clientele affirms its own racial or ethnic identity, often through its disapproving talk about others. For example, through the recollection and retelling of past negative events, Trena's patrons develop a shared racial identity. They come to understand that their negative experiences with Whites are not isolated experiences but rather are shared by many other African Americans. These accumulated experiences become the basis for a collective memory of racism and discrimination such that each story told by the patrons provides further evidence that racism and discrimination are prevalent.

The power of sharing stories and conversation with one's peers can be phenomenal, given the fact that much of how we, as individuals, come to understand the world around us is shaped by our interactions with those with whom we are in frequent association.[4] The congregation of individuals within the tavern allows them to pour forth stories of racism and discrimination that may not be welcome in other settings. This baring of the soul is a cathartic experience. By sharing their experiences with one another, African Americans bolster their confidence in their ability to deal with negative interracial conditions, instead of being adversely affected by them. For some patrons, a trip to the tavern is equivalent to a visit to the therapist. Patrons' knowledge that others have experienced what they are going through is key for the survival of self-identity, an identity intertwined with the understanding that racial conflict is something that happens every day in a world that emphasizes race.

Duality of Interracial Encounters

Far more interesting than the patrons' cathartic relief achieved in tavern talk is the knowledge that patrons' interracial experiences are not one sided. Somewhere there is a person who is responsible for an act committed against a patron that the patron has perceived as insensitive, damaging, or infuriating. There is a man or women from another time or place who called a patron "nigger," gave "shitty service," or doubted a patron's ability because of his race. The White participants who shared in the original interracial exchanges—assuming the patrons' recollections are grounded in real experience—are telling the other side of the story within their racially segregated neighborhood settings. They are having a drink at their favorite tavern, getting a haircut at the local barbershop, or simply relaxing over a hot meal with friends. In their leisure, they, too, are making sense of their encounters with African Americans. Perhaps they are recalling and retelling stories about "lazy" or "incompetent" Black workers. They may be sharing stories of the time they were accosted by a Black criminal or how they lost an opportunity to work because an unqualified African American was given the job, instead of a qualified White.

It is the concurrent talk in these separate and distinct racially homogeneous settings that facilitates the powerful paradox between the therapeutic value of race talk in informal settings and the compounding effects of such talk. While African Americans are sharing their stories of negative racial encounters, Whites are also sharing theirs. What this amounts to is a fragmentation and a reification of negative interracial experiences. As Whites and Blacks move through multiple racially segregated gathering places, they reaffirm their racial identity by highlighting the negative characteristics they attributed to each other.

Perhaps what is most troubling about discussions of negative characteristics attributed to Whites by African Americans and to African Americans by Whites is that such discussions produce an apprehensive predisposition toward members of the other group. As individuals move into interracial interactions, they come to those interactions predisposed to expect that the encounters will have a negative outcome. Entering association with others and having the expectation that things will go wrong only helps to reinforce the use of racial frames—personal perspectives that emphasize race—in viewing interracial encounters. In using these frames to view experience, individuals take little account of the particularity of each interracial interaction but, rather, rely on conceptions of an experience that are built up through race talk in racially homogeneous settings. Such practice illustrates the debilitating function of racially homogenous settings. These settings help to produce what might be thought of as the "dragging of racial tradition," or the reaffirmation of the racial status quo.

Racial Tradition and Mass Media Influence

Traditional thoughts on race relations are pulled through the generations because, even as people of different racial and ethnic groups learn more about one another, most continue to use the old racial frames of reference to interpret others' behavior in interracial encounters. Again, the use of traditional ways to look at race relations in America is not exclusive to middle-aged African American tavern patrons but extends to younger generations in segregated settings, such as the fraternity houses of predominantly White college frats, "the Black corner" of the school cafeteria, and the locker rooms of sports teams from racially segregated high schools. The perceptions of race that participants develop in these socially segregated settings are rarely challenged by outside influences such as the mass media, a key contributor to American culture.

The depiction of racial harmony on television programs, in newspapers, or over the radio air waves has done little to change personal opinions about race held by individuals in racially segregated settings. Displays of racial harmony, such as interracial dance couples on MTV's Spring Break programs, televised sporting events in which teammates of different racial backgrounds share in the glory of victory, or the presentation of interracial friendships on television sitcoms, are inconsistent with everyday *reality*. The *reality* for most is that racial harmony is a fiction. Racial harmony is such a fiction that mass media coverage of negative racial encounters, although fewer in number than the presentations of racial harmony, carry far more weight than do the subtle and obvious displays of members of different racial groups getting along. Americans' emphasis on the negative aspects of racial encounters results largely from the fact that much of what they watch, read, and hear is taken in and reinterpreted according to the recipient's own experiences. For instance, in viewing television, tavern patrons personalize the television program themes to fit their everyday experiences. Many of their experiences are grounded in the historical perception of interpersonal racial conflict created and maintained by past structural conditions of inequality and re-emphasized by present day de facto segregation. Thus, it is the patrons' *real-life* experiences that influences their interpretation of television *fantasy*.

Although both African Americans and Whites draw from their personal experiences to clarify racial themes taken from the mass media, Whites are less likely to do so because they generally have had fewer extended interpersonal interactions with Blacks.[5] Thus, Whites may more readily turn to mass media information to develop their ideas about African Americans and their behavior, attitudes, and values. This use of information from the mass media to understand African Americans is particularly troubling since media images continue to be loaded with negative racial stereotypes.[6] Still, regardless of the source of both Blacks' and Whites' negative images of one another, each group continues to use this imagery to emphasize its own racial identity, while dragging along traditional ideas of race.

In addition to providing negative racial stereotypes that may become the basis for Whites' perceptions of African Americans, the mass media also provide information that is key for how patrons and other African Americans continue to view their own circumstance. For instance, media reports of police racial profiling of African Americans—the systematic and unjust attribution of criminal behavior to African Americans and police actions taken on the basis of this characterization—revive feelings of humiliation that many African Americans have had when they were verbally or physically abused by police officers without justification. Such experiences with police brutality and harassment are so common, especially among African American men, that many African Americans *naturally* expect one another to be able to testify to the personal horrors associated with negative police treatment that they or their close friends or family members have experienced.

High-profile media reports of police brutality and harassment, like the Rodney King beating,[7] resonate through African Americans' individual and collective experiences. Although the King beating may have been perceived by the broader public as an isolated incident, it was an event that reminded many African Americans of their own experiences with police. The King beating has been followed by a continuous stream of high-profile reports regarding police brutality and general police misconduct toward racial minorities. Recent cases include the cases of Geronimo Pratt, an African American male who was falsely imprisoned by the Los Angeles police; Amadou Diallo, an unarmed West African immigrant who was shot forty-one times by White police officers; Freddie McCollum Jr., an African American who was wrongly beaten by police; and Abner Louima, a Haitian immigrant who was sodomized with a broken broomstick by a New York City police officer.[8] These occurrences emphasize racial conflict and complement the negative experiences with White police officers that so many patrons have had and conveyed to others through narrative. High-profile cases become further proof to individuals that there is in fact sustained police misconduct toward African Americans because, as one patron put it, "they come for us just 'cause we are Black."

African Americans' awareness of racial discrimination, as highlighted by mass media reports, is not limited to police brutality but extends into the broader reaches of African Americans' everyday lives. For instance, high-profile cases of discrimination in public accommodations and in the workplace help to reinforce individual experiences with racial discrimination that many African Americans have had. These cases include the $42 million discrimination suit settlement made by the Denny's Restaurant chain in 1994 to Black patrons who had allegedly received poorer services than their White counterparts and the $8 million discrimination settlement made by Adam Mark, a hotel chain that allegedly overcharged its Black guests, subjected them to stricter security measures than Whites, and provided them with inferior services.[9] Further evidence of continued discrimination against African Americans is reinforced by cases like the $212 million discrimination lawsuit settlement made by the corporate soft drink giant Coca-Cola. The Coca-Cola Corporation settled with two thousand current and former African American employees who filed a class action suit alleging that the company had treated them unfairly in pay and promotions.[10] The seemingly ceaseless flow of discrimination cases has even hit high-tech companies like Lockheed Martin, the nation's largest defense contractor, and NEC Electronics, charged with unfair treatment of African American employees.[11]

Perhaps more troubling to African Americans than the discriminatory practices of private companies are the discriminatory practices of government agencies. For instance, in 1999, African American farmers settled a discrimination lawsuit with the United States Department of Agriculture's Farm Services Agency. The settlement, $50,000 per farmer (19,191 farmers), "was intended to remedy discrimination against Black farmers who for decades had been turned down for farm loans or received loans too late to plant a profitable crop" and to compensate for these discriminatory practices, which "led to foreclosures and the loss of way of life that had existed for generations."[12] Given such practices by the U.S. government, there is little wonder that African Americans, like the regulars at Trena's, believe in the plausibility of conspiracy theories that implicate the United States government in wrongdoing aimed at Blacks.

Finally, mass media presentations of racially motivated attacks against African Americans, like that against James Byrd Jr., who was murdered by three White men in Jasper, Texas, continues to give convincing proof to African Americans that the color of one's skin matters in determining how one is treated. Such media reports of racial antagonism, merged with the individual and historical experiences of African Americans, produce a collective memory of racism and discrimination that is not easily shaken by the often superficial changes in public attitude toward African Americans. With the understanding that things *are* different *yet* the same, both African Americans and Whites continue to drag the tradition of race behind them.

Conclusion

For people of different racial and ethnic groups, racially segregated social settings, like Trena's, provide an opportune place to open up and express themselves without facing scrutiny from members of other racial and ethnic groups. In sharing their feelings with one another, the individuals within the group further develop a positive collective racial identity. Yet, the development of such a racial identity creates a paradox that negatively affects future interracial interactions. This paradox—affirming one's own racial identity while compounding negative impressions of others—must be challenged.

We, as individuals, must push through the boundaries of de facto segregation that exist where we live and play. The initiative, in part, falls to individuals from all racial and ethnic groups to push themselves beyond the comfort zone of familiar life. Taking such a step, however, presents a challenge, since the social reward for such action is small and the cost is great. Those individuals who transgress the boundaries of race or ethnicity become victims of powerful social taboos that continue to demarcate racial and ethnic lines. Such individuals are frequently frowned on as "sellouts" or "crossovers." Very few people can withstand the implicit and explicit social pressure that constrains them to be with people who are like themselves.

Perhaps sustained incentives created by broader American sociopolitical institutions would help move individuals and groups to take action toward achieving greater racial harmony through an appreciation of others' differences. After all, it was the historical power of these same sociopolitical institutions that created the current antagonistic relationships between people of different racial and ethnic groups. If we fail to offer incentives via sociopolitical institutions that facilitate interpersonal experiences with diverse others, we are destined to drag the tradition of racial and ethnic conflict behind us and drag this country down with it.

APPENDIX

Gathering Data

Developing an intimate understanding of a social world often requires an ethnographer to jump headlong, with little theoretical restraint, into participation and observation of the social world to be studied. I did just that by becoming a regular at Trena's, visiting Trena's three to four times per week over an eighteen-month period. As soon as possible after each visit, usually within fifteen minutes, I reconstructed, from memory, my observations of patrons' interactions. During some visits, I would "run" to the rest room, claiming an urgent need to relieve myself, in order to record sketchy notes of the events that I had witnessed. I later referred to these sketchy notes to assist my memory during detailed reconstruction of field events. Since no mechanical recording device was used to capture patrons' conversations, I must caution that the notes presented are representative of the general spirit of discourse in the tavern, rather than verbatim transcriptions of patrons' comments. Nevertheless, this methodological approach is consistent with that used in traditional ethnographic studies and is a trusted way to gather information about informal social settings.

Recording devices, although they provide an accurate replication of dialogue, are often viewed as obtrusive by subjects and researchers alike. Most participants in informal settings would significantly alter their behavior if they were constantly reminded that their behavior was being recorded. For this reason, I avoided the use of a tape recorder.

Trena's and the Ethnographer "Me"

My goal as an ethnographer was to document the daily lifestyle of Trena's regulars, while being as unobtrusive as possible. This meant that my research objectives were rarely a salient topic of tavern discussion. Instead, I spent most of my time listening to the patrons' exchanges and documenting those topics patrons thought important. This technique of low-key involvement yielded a number of observations. Occasionally, Monique, the bartender, would remind the patrons in the tavern that I was studying them. Her reminders had little effect on the patrons after a few weeks, because most of them were aware of my multiple roles as a student, researcher, father, husband, and native Chicagoan. Perhaps their pride in my achievements as a young African American male made them willing participants in my research endeavor. As the patrons accepted me as a regular, I came to understand that my identity outside the tavern was less important than the identity I established within the tavern. In reconstructing my daily observations from the field, I also became aware of the relative ease with which I participated in tavern social interactions.

Two identity characteristics facilitated my easy interaction with the regulars. First, I was of the same race and gender as the patrons who frequented the tavern. Despite being younger than most regulars, I shared many experiences related to their lives as African American men. For instance, when patrons recalled stories of being looked on by others as a threatening Black male, I could understand their feelings, since I had had similar experiences myself.

The second characteristic that eased my interaction with the regulars was my status as a husband. Many of the patrons had experienced or were experiencing issues common to marriage. We were able to share stories of the joys and pains of marriage, and the men offered ways to think about relationships that I noted for my own use. They reiterated simple themes, such as respect for one's spouse. These ideas were worthy of being remembered on days when I struggled with the complexity of marriage myself. As I talked about my personal life struggles with the patrons, my life became intertwined with the social life of those at the tavern in much the same way that the other patrons' lives had. Our shared status made Trena's a place where we could go to make sense of the world and to understand one another.

For the same reasons that my marital status and my race and gender provided me with useful background knowledge for interaction and understanding at Trena's, my age was one limitation. Many of the men were twenty years my elder and talked about their lives within a historical context. I recognized my limited life experience early on in the research and frequently asked specific questions about the historical contexts of the events the patrons described. The regulars were more than happy to answer my questions. In many ways, my limited historical knowledge of their experiences made the study much more interesting. I could rarely assume that I understood the contexts of patrons' recollections.

My interaction in Trena's was also limited by my lack of work experience and by the type of work that I had done. I had worked full-time for only a few years of my life, and those experiences included employment as a busboy, dishwasher, waiter, and social worker. Many of Trena's patrons had worked as skilled laborers (e.g., plumbers and electricians), as well as in manufacturing jobs. Their experiences at work were outside my knowledge of work. Again, the probing questions I asked about their work produced rich answers.

Despite my personal limitations, my role as a participant observer in Trena's generated substantial data about patrons' everyday attitudes and lifestyles. More important, my time at Trena's allowed me to share a life experience with a group of regulars—an experience that has been far more enriching personally than the research itself.

Television and Race Considerations

I faced at least two interrelated limitations in gathering data concerning patrons' incorporation of racial thematic content from television. First, as indicated in chapter 3, observations of patrons' interaction and their viewing of television were made around noon and during the early evening hours. In this way, intimate details of interaction could be recorded without the clamor and fast-paced, superficial, and anonymous conversation associated with late-night use of the tavern.

Second, my choice of afternoon and early evening for studying social interaction limited the range of television themes I could observe the patrons using in their conversation. During the afternoon and early evening hours, television programming usually and narrowly included talk shows, soap operas, tabloid news programs, game shows, and music videos. Missing from such a lineup are the programs that "seriously" consider issues of race, such as documentaries and prime-time news programs. Thus, the patrons' commentary about television was limited to the topics provided by "entertainment" television.

Patrons' Beliefs, Attitudes, and Behavior

Throughout the text, I refer to patrons' or regulars' beliefs, attitudes, and behavior. Although I use the broad designates of *patrons* or *regulars*, I do not mean to suggest that all of the individual patrons within the tavern were necessarily in agreement about a particular set of beliefs, attitudes, or behaviors. Instead, I use the plural possessive to indicate a particular moral order that represents the consensus among a core group of patrons. Still, to impute beliefs, attitudes, or behaviors to a particular group of people on the basis of what they say is a risky endeavor.

It may be that the ways in which I have interpreted patrons' attitudes, beliefs, and behavior are inconsistent with what the men and women really have thought, felt, or said, because *reality* is a constantly shifting phenomenon for individuals and groups alike. That *reality* is based on a number of factors, including broader contexts and individual idiosyncracies.[1] Thus, my generalizations about tavern patrons' beliefs, attitudes, and behavior are grounded in my interpretation of the contexts in which patrons' talk occurred and in my own experience. This raises the following question: if the interpretation of others' *reality* is subjective, should we, as researchers, shy away from interpreting their behavior? The answer must be no. Everyday life is rife with misinterpretation. Despite these miscues, individuals continue to share in social relations with others, which in turn helps them to develop common understandings that reduce the likelihood of error. Still, misinterpretations are a social fact. For my part, I have written this book knowing that if I have erred in conveying patrons' beliefs, attitudes, and behaviors, I have done so with the confidence that I would have interpreted the patrons' lives in much the same way had Trena's been my own place of escape.

NOTES

Notes to Introduction

1. All names of places and people are pseudonyms.

2. See Sherri Cavan, *Liquor License: An Ethnography of Bar Behavior* (Chicago: Aldine, 1966) and E. E. LeMasters, *Blue-Collar Aristocrat: Life-styles at a Working-Class Tavern* (Madison: University of Wisconsin Press, 1975).

3. See Elijah Anderson, *A Place on the Corner* (Chicago: University of Chicago Press, 1978).

4. See Michael Bell, *The World from Brown's Lounge: An Ethnography of Black Middle-Class Play* (Urbana: University of Illinois Press, 1983).

5. See Ray Oldenburg, *The Great Good Place: Cafés, Coffee Shops, Community Centers, Beauty Parlors, General Stores, Bars, Hangouts, and How They Get You through the Day* (New York: Marlowe, [1989] 1997).

6. See Anderson, *A Place*, chapter 6.

7. See Linda Waite, "Does Marriage Matter?" *Demography* 32(4) (November 1995): 483–507.

8. For further discussion of the "ethnographic present" see R. Lincoln Keiser, *The Vice Lords: Warriors of the Streets* (New York: Holt, Rinehart and Winston, 1969), chapter 1.

9. The last visit was in August 2000.

Notes to Chapter 1

1. For a description of the rapid racial change in communities surrounding South Gate see Mary Pattillo-McCoy, *Black Picket Fences: Privilege and Peril among the Black Middle Class* (Chicago: University of Chicago Press, 1999), chapter 1.

2. For a discussion of the bartender's role in social interaction see Michael Bell, *The World from Brown's Lounge: An Ethnography of Black Middle Class Play*, (Chicago: University of Illinois Press, 1983); James Spradley and Brenda Mann, *The Cocktail Waitress: Woman's Work in a Man's World* (New York: Wiley, 1975); and E. E. LeMasters, *Blue-Collar Aristocrats: Life-styles at a Working-Class Tavern* (Madison: University of Wisconsin Press, 1975).

3. For a discussion of tavern language and culture see Sherri Cavan, *Liquor License: An Ethnography of Bar Behavior* (Chicago: Aldine, 1966); Bell, *Brown's Lounge*, 17–32; Elijah Anderson, *A Place on the Corner* (Chicago: University of Chicago Press, 1978); Michael Katovich and William Reese II, "The Regular: Full-time Identities and Membership in an Urban Bar," *Journal of Contemporary Ethnography* 16 (1987): 308–343.

4. For a discussion of increased opportunities for Blacks see William J. Wilson, *The Declining Significance of Race: Blacks and Changing American Institutions*, 2d ed. (Chicago: University of Chicago Press, 1980); William J. Wilson, *The Truly Disadvantaged: The Inner City, the Underclass and Public Policy* (Chicago: University of Chicago Press, 1987).

5. For a discussion of reading behavioral cues in public spaces see Elijah Anderson, *Code of the Street: Decency, Violence, and the Moral Life of the Inner City* (New York: Norton, 1999), 134.

6. For a discussion of conflict that results as gang members mark off their territory from rival gangs through symbols such as hats see Felix

Padilla, *The Gang as an American Enterprise* (New Brunswick: Rutgers University Press, 1992), chapter 3. For a discussion of the crime and gang problems that some middle-class African Americans confront because they live near high-poverty areas see Pattillo-McCoy, *Black Picket Fences,* chapter 6.

7. Bell, *Brown's Lounge,* 17–36.

8. For a discussion of "facework" see Erving Goffman, *Interaction Ritual: Essays in Face-to-Face Behavior* (Chicago: Aldine, 1967), chapter 1.

9. Bell, *Brown's Lounge,* chapter 1; LeMasters, *Blue-Collar Aristocrat,* 147–151; and Cavan, *Liquor License.*

10. For a discussion of creative self-expression in tavern settings see Bell, *Brown's Lounge,* 108–135.

Notes to Chapter 2

1. See Mary Pattillo-McCoy, *Black Picket Fences: Privilege and Peril among the Black Middle Class* (Chicago: University of Chicago Press, 1999), chapters 1 and 2.

2. See for example David Halle, *America's Working Man: Work, Home, and Politics among Blue-Collar Property Owners* (Chicago: University of Chicago Press, 1984), chapter 1; Michael Katovich and William Reese II, "The Regular: Full-time Identities and Membership in an Urban Bar," *Journal of Contemporary Ethnography* 16 (1987): 308–343; and E. E. LeMasters, *Blue-Collar Aristocrats: Life-styles at a Working-Class Tavern* (Madison: University of Wisconsin Press, 1975).

3. For a discussion of African Americans' class self-conception, see how residents of Groveland, a middle-class African American neighborhood that shares its boundaries with South Gate, identify themselves in Pattillo-McCoy, *Black Picket Fences,* 13–30.

4. Patrons today, like many other Americans, use a much broader definition of middle class than was used in the past. For a discussion of the wide range of definitions for working class and middle class see Halle, *America's Working Man,* ppxi–xviii. Even within the middle class, African Americans make distinctions (e.g., "ghetto" or "country") that are related to cultural phenomena. For a discussion of such distinctions see Pattillo-McCoy, *Black Picket Fences,* chapter 1.

5. For a discussion of the increased prosperity of African Americans

see for example William J. Wilson, *When Work Disappears: The World of the New Urban Poor* (New York: Knopf, 1996); Reynolds Farley and Walter R. Allen, *The Color Line and the Quality of American Life* (New York: Russell Sage Foundation, 1987); Mary Corcoran and Sharon Parrot, "African American Women's Economic Progress," in *African American and Latina Women at Work: Race, Gender, and Economic Inequality* (New York: Russell Sage, 1998); and Pattillo-McCoy, *Black Picket Fences*. All suggest that, while the Black middle class has increased in size and prosperity, it still lags behind the White middle class in categories such as income and home ownership.

6. There are several studies devoted to the mass migration of Blacks from North to South during this time period. See for example St. Clair Drake and Horace Cayton, *Black Metropolis: A Study of Negro Life in a Northern City*, revised and enlarged (Chicago: University of Chicago Press, [1945] 1993); Nicholas Lemann, *The Promised Land: The Great Black Migration and How It Changed America* (New York: Vintage Books, 1991); Carol Marks, *Farewell—We're Good and Gone* (Bloomington: Indiana University Press, 1989); and Allan H. Spear, *Black Chicago: The Making of a Negro Ghetto: 1890–1920* (Chicago: University of Chicago Press, 1967).

7. For a discussion of the economic and social fragility of the Black middle class see Sharon M. Collins, "Blacks on the Bubble: The Vulnerability of Black Executives in White Corporations," *Sociological Quarterly* 34 (1993): 429–447; Melvin L. Oliver and Thomas M. Shapiro, *Black Wealth/White Wealth: A New Perspective on Racial Inequality* (New York: Routledge, 1995); and Farley and Allen, *The Color Line*.

8. For a comparative analysis of Black and White wealth see Oliver and Shapiro, *Black Wealth*, and Farai Chideya, *Don't Believe the Hype: Fighting Cultural Misinformation about African-Americans* (New York: Plume, 1995), 116–120.

9. According to Oliver and Shapiro (1995) African Americans remain in a "precarious-resource" circumstance even when they are employed. In fact, 78.9 percent of Black households, compared to only 38.1 percent of White households, do not have adequate financial assets or net worth to survive three months of poverty if they were suddenly unemployed. Thus, sudden unemployment can have a more immediate and profound overall effect on African American households than on White households.

10. For a discussion of the disproportionate location of middle-class African Americans among urban poor see Douglass Massey, Gretchen A. Condran, and Nancy A. Denton, "The Effect of Residential Segregation on Black Social and Economic Well-Being," *Social Forces* 66 (1987): 29–57.

11. Wilson suggests that competition in the labor market has held wages down and many long-time employees are opting to hold onto their jobs because jobs with insufficient pay are better than no jobs. See William J. Wilson, *Over the Racial Divide: Rising Inequality and Coalition Politics* (Berkeley: University of California Press, 1999), 59–66.

12. See Elijah Anderson, *A Place on the Corner* (Chicago: University of Chicago Press, 1978), 28–29.

13. For example, see Anderson, *A Place*, for a discussion of the tension created within a tavern when patrons are both employed working class and unemployed lower class. Also see William J. Wilson, *The Truly Disadvantaged: The Inner City, the Underclass and Public Policy* (Chicago: University of Chicago Press), 1987, chapter 3, for an examination of the effects of high poverty and social isolation on the social institutions and individuals of those communities.

Notes to Chapter 3

1. The use of the term *genre* follows William Bielby and Denise Bielby, "All Hits Are Flukes," *American Journal of Sociology* 99(5) (1994): 1287–1313. "Television genres are conventions regarding the content of television series—formulas that prescribe format, themes, premises, characterizations, etc." (p. 1292).

2. "Gangsta rap" is a form of rap music that most often carries violent themes of inner-city street life. These themes include violent attacks against others, gang life, abuse of women, and crime. This particular rap video was not concerned with "gangsta rap." For a discussion of gangsta rap see Edward Armstrong, "The Rhetoric of Violence in Rap and Country Music," *Sociological Inquiry* 63(1) (1993): 64–83; and Tricia Rose, *Black Noise: Rap Music and Black Culture in Contemporary America* (Hanover, N.H.: Wesleyan University Press, 1994).

3. For a discussion of moral order see Gerald Suttles, *The Social Order of the Slum: Ethnicity and Territory in the Inner City* (Chicago:

University of Chicago Press, 1968); and Mitchell Duneier, *Slim's Table: Race, Respectability and Masculinity* (Chicago: University of Chicago, 1992).

4. As John Fiske, *Television Culture* (London: Methuen, 1987), demonstrates in his study of television culture, "All popular audiences engage in varying degrees of semiotic productivity, producing meanings and pleasures that pertain to their social situation out of products of the cultural industries" (p. 30). See also John Fiske, "The Cultural Economy of Fandom," in *The Adoring Audience: Fan Culture and Popular Media*, edited by L. Lewis (New York: Routledge, 1992), 30–49; Joshua Gamson, *Claims to Fame: Celebrity in Contemporary America* (Berkeley: University of California Press, 1994); Marie Gillespie, *Television, Ethnicity, and Cultural Change* (New York: Routledge, 1995); Henry Jenkins, *Textual Poachers: Television Fans and Participatory Culture* (London: Routledge, 1992); and David Morley, *Nationwide Audience* (London: British Film Institute, 1980).

5. For a discussion of reciprocity in interpersonal relations see Georg Simmel, *On Individuality and Social Forms* (reprint) (Chicago: University of Chicago Press, [1910] 1971).

6. For a more thorough description of parasocial relationships see David Horton and Robert Wohl, "Mass Communication and Parasocial Interaction," *Psychiatry* 19 (1956): 215–224; Elizabeth Perse and Rebecca Rubin, "Attribution in Social and Parasocial Relationships," *Communication Research* 16 (1989): 59–77; and John Jensen, "Fandom as Pathology: The Consequences of Characterization." in *The Adoring Audience: Fan Culture and Popular Media*, edited by L. Lewis (New York: Routledge, 1992), 9–29.

7. For a discussion of television programs as a social link see Denise Bielby and C. Harrington, "Reach Out and Touch Someone: Viewers, Agency, and Audiences in the Televisual Experience," in *Viewing, Reading, Listening*, edited by J. Cruz and J. Lewis (Boulder, Colo.: Westview, 1994), 81–100.

8. Individuals develop greater intimacy with television persona as they view them over time. For a discussion of this increased intimacy with television persona see David Lemish, "Soap Opera Viewing in College: A Naturalistic Inquiry," *Journal of Broadcasting and Electronic Media* 29 (1985): 275–293.

9. Melvin is a comedy character from radio who offers daily updates

of TV soaps. He presents himself as a gossipy beautician with a high voice and feminine mannerisms.

10. For a discussion of the intended audience of soap operas see Dorothy Hobson, "Housewives and the Mass Media," in *Culture, Media, Language,* edited by S. Hall, D. Hobson, A. Lowe, and P. Willis (London: Unwin Hyman, 1980), 105–114; and T. Modleski, *Loving with a Vengeance: Mass-Produced Fantasies for Women* (New York: Routledge, 1982).

11. Trena's patrons share in the traditionally held working class values like those expressed in David Halle, *America's Working Man: Work, Home, and Politics among Blue-Collar Property Owners* (Chicago: University of Chicago Press, 1984); and E. E. LeMasters, *Blue-Collar Aristocrat: Life-styles at a Working-Class Tavern* (Madison: University of Wisconsin Press, 1975).

12. The significance of celebrity gossip and moral standing is discussed in David Altheide and Robert Snow, *Media Worlds in the Postjournalism Era* (New York: Aldine, 1991), who state, "Indeed, much of what goes on in entertainment TV is identical to interpersonal gossip, and gossip is directly concerned with the moral fabric of society. Everyone gossips to some degree, and in doing so comparisons are made between self and others on the rules and values that matter in society" (p. 45).

13. For a discussion of "front stage" and "back stage" performance see Erving Goffman, *Presentations of Self in Everyday Life* (New York: Anchor Books, 1959).

14. For a discussion of media influence on the conceptions of African American males see Elijah Anderson, *Streetwise: Race, Class, and Change in an Urban Community* (Chicago: University of Chicago Press, 1990) and Duneier, *Slim's Table,* chapter 9.

15. See Christopher B. Smith, "Back and to the Future: The Intergroup Contact Hypothesis Revisited," *Sociological Inquiry* 64(4) (November 1994): 438–455.

Notes to Chapter 4

1. For a thorough discussion of neighborhood segregation not only in Chicago but in other metropolitan areas throughout the U.S. see Douglass Massey and Nancy Denton, *American Apartheid:*

Segregation and the Making of the Underclass (Cambridge, Mass.: Harvard University Press, 1993). Massey and Denton argue that hypersegregation—the segregation, clustering, and isolation of African Americans from other groups—is largely due to historical discrimination and the racially restricted housing market. These set in motion a continuous trend of segregation as a result of which African Americans live in close proximity to one another, on the smallest areas of land, and near the central city in the most economically depressed areas.

2. For a comparative perspective on both African Americans' views of Whites and Whites' views of African Americans see Mia Bay, *The White Image in the Black Mind: African-American Ideas about White People, 1830–1925* (New York: Oxford University Press, 2000); and George Fredrickson, *The Black Image in the White Mind: The Debate on Afro-American Character and Destiny, 1817–1914* (New York: Harper and Row, 1977; reprinted, Middletown, Conn.: Wesleyan University Press, 1987).

3. Although there have been challenges to the notion of a core black culture, John Gwaltney argues that African Americans have developed a core black culture as an adaptive response to their common experience of oppression. See John Gwaltney, *Drylongso: A Self-Portrait of Black America* (New York: Random House, 1980).

4. For a discussion of the gains made by African Americans see William J. Wilson, *The Declining Significance of Race,* 2d ed. (Chicago: University of Chicago Press, 1980), and *The Truly Disadvantaged: The Inner City, the Underclass and Public Policy* (Chicago: University of Chicago Press, 1987).

5. For a discussion of restricted housing markets see Massey and Denton, *American Apartheid.* For a discussion of the economic and social influence that the migration of southern Blacks to the north had on America see Nicholas Lemann, *The Promised Land: The Great Black Migration and How It Changed America* (New York: Knopf, 1991).

6. For a discussion of the attitudes regarding racial inferiority see Howard Schuman, Charlotte Steeh, and Lawrence Bobo, *Racial Attitudes in America: Trends and Interpretations* (Cambridge, Mass.: Harvard University Press, 1985). Arguments supporting the notion of intellectual inferiority based on race and class are resurfacing. For example, see Charles Murray and Richard Herrnstein, *The Bell Curve:*

Intelligence and Class Structure in American Life (New York: Simon and Schuster, 1994) and Dinesh D'Souza, *The End of Racism: Principles of a Multiracial Society* (New York: Free Press, 1995).

7. For one African American's confrontation with questions of racial inferiority and Affirmative Action see Stephen Carter, *Reflections of an Affirmative Action Baby* (New York: Basic Books, 1991). In part, Carter argues that affirmative action programs have stigmatized capable African Americans as incapable and that such programs should therefore be eliminated.

8. For a discussion of how middle-class African Americans cope with Whites' challenges to Black middle-class status see Joe Feagin and Melvin P. Sikes, *Living with Racism: The Black Middle Class Experience* (Boston: Beacon Press, 1994).

9. Despite South Gate residents' ability to travel outside the community for those goods and services they desire, many of them use the goods and services provided by the numerous businesses on Eighth Avenue. Eighth Avenue serves as the business center for several of the Black neighborhoods annexed to South Gate. For a discussion of these neighborhoods and their connection to South Gate see Mary Pattillo-McCoy, *Black Picket Fences: Privilege and Peril among the Black Middle Class* (Chicago: University of Chicago Press, 1999), chapter 2.

10. Elijah Anderson, an urban sociologist, refers to this process of attributing criminality to African Americans as "color-coding." See Elijah Anderson, *Streetwise: Race, Class, and Change in an Urban Community* (Chicago: University of Chicago Press, 1990), chapter 7. Anderson states:

> On the streets, color-coding often works to confuse race, age, class, gender, incivility, and criminality, and it expresses itself most concretely in the person of the anonymous black male. In doing their job, the police often become willing parties to this general color-coding of the public environment, and related distinctions, particularly those of skin color and gender, come to convey definite meanings. . . . Moreover, the anonymous black male is usually an ambiguous figure who arouses the utmost caution and is generally considered dangerous until he proves he is not. (p. 190)

11. The racial profiling of African Americans by police has long been

a topic of discussion among African Americans. *Jet* magazine, one of the oldest and most widely read weekly periodicals among African Americans, has presented several stories regarding racial profiling, police brutality, and general police misconduct. See, for example, a report that asserts that police use racial profiling to stop and detain Blacks and Hispanics: "Civil Rights Commission Cites Improper Use of Racial Profiling by New York City Police," *Jet*, vol. 98 no. 4 (July 3, 2000); the case of Geronimo Pratt, who was falsely imprisoned by the Los Angeles police, in Silvia P. Flanagan, ed., "Falsely Imprisoned Ex-Black Panther 'Geronimo' Pratt to Get 4.5 Million in Settlement," *Jet*, vol. 97, no. 23 (May 15, 2000); the story of the acquittal of four white officers who shot Amadou Diallo, an unarmed West African immigrant, forty-one times, "Four White Officers Acquitted in New York's Diallo Shooting Case; Blacks Protest Verdicts," *Jet*, vol. 97, no. 15 (March 13, 2000); the case of Freddie McCollum Jr., who was beaten so badly by Prince George's County police that he lost his right eye and suffered a broken leg, two cracked ribs, and numerous other injuries, "Police Brutality Settlement," *Jet*, vol. 97, no. 20 (April 24, 2000) and the story of Abner Louima, a Haitian immigrant, who was sodomized by a New York police officer with a broken broomstick, "Ex-New York Cop Gets 15 Years in Louima Torture Case," *Jet*, vol. 98, no. 6 (July 17, 2000). These stories reiterate the reality through which patrons and other African Americans view their everyday interaction with police, in particular White police officers.

12. For a discussion of how individuals develop cultural repertoires to confront the complexities of everyday life see Ulf Hannerz, *Soul Side: Inquiries into Ghetto Culture and Community* (New York: Columbia University Press, 1969). The notion of cultural repertoire is given conceptual clarity in Ann Swidler, "Culture in Action: Symbols and Strategies," *American Sociological Review* 51 (1986): 273–286.

13. See Michael Bell, *The World from Brown's Lounge: An Ethnography of Black Middle-Class Play* (University of Illinois, Press, 1983), 17–36.

14. See Charisse Jones, "Race Killing in Texas Fuels Fear and Anger," *USA Today*, June 11, 1998, p. 1A.

15. For a discussion of African Americans' use of conspiracy theories see Theodore Sasson, "African American Conspiracy Theories and the Social Construction of Crime," *Sociological Inquiry* 65 (3/4) (1995): 265–285; and Anita Waters, "Conspiracy Theories as Ethnosociologies:

Explanation and Intention in African American Political Culture," *Journal of Black Studies* 28(1) (1997): 112–125.

16. *JFK* (1991), Oliver Stone (director), stars Kevin Costner and Tommy Lee Jones; *Enemy of the State* (1998), Tony Scott (director), stars Will Smith and Gene Hackman.

17. See Paul Farmer, *AIDS and Accusation: Haiti and the Geography of Blame* (Berkeley: University of California Press, 1992); Terry Ann Knopf, *Rumors, Race, and Riots* (New Brunswick, N.J.: Transaction Books, 1975); and Patricia Turner, *I Heard It through the Grapevine: Rumor in African American Culture* (Berkeley: University of California Press, 1993).

18. Turner, *Grapevine*, 9–32.

19. Some commentators have judged the use of conspiracy theories paranoid or delusional. For a discussion of conspiracy theories as delusional or paranoid see Richard Hofstadter, "The Paranoid Style in American Politics," in *The Fear of Conspiracy: Images of Un-American Subversion from the Revolution to the Present*, edited by David B. Davis (Ithaca, N.Y.: Cornell University Press, 1971), 2–8; Dieter Groh, "The Temptation of Conspiracy Theory, or: Why Do Bad Things Happen to Good People?" in *Changing Conceptions of Conspiracy*, edited by Carl F. Graumann and Serge Moscovici (New York: Springer-Verlag, 1987), 1–37; and Erich Wulff, "Paranoic Conspiratory Delusion," in *Changing Conceptions of Conspiracy*, edited by Carl F. Graumann and Serge Moscovici (New York: Springer-Verlag, 1987), 177–190.

20. African Americans' belief in conspiracy theories is fueled by past conspiracies against African Americans, such as the Federal Bureau of Investigation's (FBI) operations against civil rights workers and the Tuskegee, Alabama, syphilis study, in which treatment was withheld from four hundred sick Black men. See James Jones, *Bad Blood: The Tuskegee Syphilis Experiment* (New York: Free Press, 1993); and Waters, "Conspiracy Theories," 122.

21. *The Godfather* (1972), Francis Ford Coppola (director), stars Marlon Brando and Al Pacino.

22. For details of the sexual abuse charge and out-of-court settlement see Bernard Weinraub, "Michael Jackson Settles Suit for Sum Said to Be in Millions," *New York Times*, January 26, 1994, Section A, page 1.

23. For a description of the Susan Smith case see Elizabeth Gleick, "Sex, Betrayal and Murder," *Time* 146 (July 1995) (3).

24. For example, in a national telephone survey of four hundred African Americans, Waters found that 57 percent of the believers had some college trade school education or more, whereas 59 percent of those skeptics of conspiracy theories had a high school diploma or less. Waters, "Conspiracy Theories," 118.

25. "John Henryism," or African Americans' notion that their poor individual performance negatively effects how others perceive African Americans' performance as a group is discussed in Roy Brooks, *Rethinking The American Race Problem* (Berkeley: University of California Press, 1990), 40–43.

26. Charles uses an African American vernacular as a way to identify with other African Americans. His use of African American vernacular is an important force unifying him and the other patrons. It authenticates Charles as a "true brother" like themselves who can "go ghetto on you." The cultural significance of Black vernacular among African Americans is so evident that many school-age African American children are teased if they use standard English because to their peers they are "acting White." Since Charles is discussing African Americans in a racially homogeneous setting, he identifies with the other patrons, using language cues with which others can readily identify. Here Charles demonstrates the ability to "code switch." See Anderson, *Streetwise*, chapter 6. That is, he uses the appropriate verbal and gestural communication techniques within the tavern; at the same time, he has the ability to speak standard English outside the tavern. To the other patrons Charles is showing his "Black side"—behavior expected in the tavern. For a discussion of social pressure to use Black English vernacular see Signithia Fordham and John Ogbu, "Black Students Success and Coping with the Burden of Acting White," *Urban Review* 18 (1986): 176–206.

Notes to Chapter 5

1. The rate of marriage has decreased for both Blacks and Whites, but Blacks have seen a far greater decrease in the past forty years. For example, in 1993 61 percent of Black women and 58 percent of Black men were not married, compared with 38 percent of White men and 41 percent of White women. See Linda Waite, "Does Marriage Matter?" *Demography* 32(4) (1995):483–507.

2. For a description of the trends toward greater cohabitation see Frances Goldscheider and Linda Waite, *New Families, No Families?: The Transformation of the American Home* (Berkeley: University of California Press, 1991).

3. For a discussion of economic changes that increase marital conflict see Stacy Rogers and Paul Amato, "Is Marital Quality Declining? The Evidence from Two Generations," *Social Forces* 75(3) (March 1997): 1089–1100.

4. The difficulty of supporting a family on a single income is especially felt among African American families of every description, which earn significantly less than White families. See Farai Chideya, *Don't Believe the Hype: Fighting Cultural Misinformation about African-Americans* (New York: Plume, 1995).

5. Little effort is necessary to maintain the tavern as a racially segregated tavern, since Whites, if given a direct invitation to Trena's, would probably turn it down in a socially acceptable manner. It is in this way that racially segregated places, in a variety of segregated neighborhoods, are maintained.

6. For a discussion of the health and financial benefits of marriage see Waite, "Does Marriage Matter?"

7. For a discussion of changes in the family see Judy A. Root, *Changing Families* (Belmont, Calif.: Wadsworth, 1994); Daphne Spain and Suzanne M. Bianchi, *Balancing Act: Motherhood, Marriage, and Employment among American Women* (New York: Russell Sage Foundation, 1996).

8. For a discussion of the wage differential between men and women see June O'Neill and Solomon Polachek, "Why the Gender Gap in Wages Narrowed in the 1980s," *Journal of Labor Economics* 11 (1993): 205–228; and Alison J. Wellington, "The Male/Female Wage Gap among Whites: 1976 and 1985," *American Sociological Review* 59 (1994): 839–848.

Notes to Chapter 6

1. See Michael Bell, *The World from Brown's Lounge: An Ethnography of Black Middle-Class Play* (Chicago: University of Illinois Press, 1983), chapter 8 discussion of "talking shit."

2. For a discussion of jokes as a means to address sensitive topics see

Murray S. Davis, *What's So Funny? The Comic Conception of Culture and Society* (Chicago: University of Chicago Press, 1993); and Larry R. Smeltzer and Terry Leap, "An Analysis of Individual Reactions to Potentially Offensive Jokes in Work Settings," *Human Relations* 41(4) (April 1988): 295–304.

3. For a discussion of the great alienation among gays in general and Black gays specifically see Leon E. Pettiway, *Honey, Honey Miss Thang: Being Black, Gay and on the Streets* (Philadelphia: Temple University Press, 1996); also William Hawkeswood, edited by Alex Costley, *One of the Children: Gay Black Men in Harlem* (Berkeley: University of California Press, 1996).

4. For a discussion of how the African body was objectified see Patricia Turner, *I Heard It through the Grapevine: Rumor in African American Culture* (Berkeley: University of California Press, 1993).

Notes to Chapter 7

1. See Ray Oldenburg, *The Great Good Place: Cafés, Coffee Shops, Community Centers, Beauty Parlors, General Stores, Bars, Hangouts, and How They Get You through the Day* (New York: Marlowe, [1989] 1997), p.16.

2. See Clifford Broman, Harold Neighbors, and James Jackson, "Racial Group Identification among Black Adults," *Social Forces* 67 (1988): 146–158.

3. See Douglass Massey and Nancy Denton, *American Apartheid: Segregation and the Making of the Underclass* (Cambridge, Mass.: Harvard University Press, 1993).

4. For a discussion of this classic notion see Herbert Blumer, *Symbolic Interactionism: Perspective and Method* (Berkeley: University of California Press, 1987).

5. The fact that African Americans are a smaller proportion of the total population than are Whites contributes to their lack of sustained interracial contact with Whites. Additionally, the added dimension of residential segregation further reduces Whites' contact with African Americans. For a discussion of the extent to which Whites' contact with Blacks is limited see L. Sigelman and S. Welch, "The Contact Hypothesis Revisited: Black-White Interaction and Positive Racial Attitudes," *Social Forces* 71(3) (1993): 781–795; and Christopher B. Smith, "Back

and to the Future: The Intergroup Contact Hypothesis Revisited," *Sociological Inquiry* 64(4)(1994): 438–455.

6. For a discussion of the continued use of Black stereotypes in the mass media see Mitchell Duneier, *Slim's Table: Race, Respectability and Masculinity* (Chicago: University of Chicago, 1992), chapter 9; Sherryl Browne Graves, "Television and Prejudice Reduction: When Does Television as a Vicarious Experience Make a Difference?" *Journal of Social Issues* 55(4) (Winter 1999): 707–727; Sheila T. Murphy, "The Impact of Factual versus Fictional Media Portrayals on Cultural Stereotypes," *Annals of the American Academy of Political and Social Science* 560 (November 1998): 165–178; Shawna V. Hudson, "Recreational television: The Paradox of Change and Continuity within Stereotypical Iconography," *Sociological Inquiry* 68(2) (1998): 242–57; Chris Grover and Keith Soothill, "Ethnicity, The Search for Rapists and the Press," *Ethnic and Racial Studies* (19) (July 1996): 567–584; Mark Peffley, Todd Shields, and Bruce Williams, "The Intersection of Race and Crime in Television News Stories: An Experimental Study," *Political Communication* 13 (July–September 1996): 309–327; and Mary Beth Oliver, "Caucasian Viewers' Memory of Black and White Criminal Suspects in the News," *Journal of Communication* 49(3) (Summer 1999): 46–60.

7. Rodney King, an African American unemployed construction worker, was pulled over by the Los Angeles police after King allegedly led them on a high-speed chase. King was then beaten by several officers and suffered numerous injuries. King's case was made high profile by the fact that witnesses to the events videotaped the officers, who struck King more than fifty times with batons and gave him electric shock from a Taser gun. This case became the impetus for a review of police conduct with regard to the use of force, racial profiling, and officer integrity in cities throughout the United States. For a discussion of the case and how it changed perceptions of police behavior see Lou Cannon, *Official Negligence: How Rodney King and the Riots Changed Los Angeles and the LAPD* (New York: Times Books, 1997).

8. For a detailed discussion of these events see "Civil Rights Commission Cites Improper Use of Racial Profiling by New York City Police," *Jet*, vol. 98, no. 4 (July 3, 2000); Silvia P. Flanagan, ed., "Falsely Imprisoned Ex-Black Panther 'Geronimo' Pratt to Get 4.5 Million in Settlement," *Jet*, vol. 97, no. 23 (May 15, 2000), 12; "Four White Officers Acquitted in New York's Diallo Shooting Case: Blacks Protest

Verdicts," *Jet*, vol. 97, no. 15 (March 13, 2000); "Police Brutality Settlement," *Jet*, vol. 97, no. 20 (April 24, 2000); and "Ex-New York Cop Gets 15 Years in Louima Torture Case," *Jet*, vol. 98, no. 6 (July 17, 2000).

9. While lawsuit settlements may provide little clear indication of wrongdoing, it is noteworthy that many corporations avoid trials. This suggests that there may be substantial evidence that would sway public sentiment to the victims of the wrongdoing and thereby cost corporations far more than pretrial settlements. For a discussion of the Denny's and the Adam Mark cases, as well as discussion of racial discrimination in other public accommodations, see "Denny's Manager Accused of Racial Bias," *Los Angeles Times*, January 8, 1998, A16; and "Full Schedule, Funding Fuel Hopes for Black College Reunion's Success; $8 Million Hotel Settlement, Corporate Contributions Help Offset Skepticism," *Baltimore Sun*, March 27, 2000, 7A.

10. For a discussion of the Coca-Cola discrimination case see Justin Bachman, "Coca-Cola to Pay Discrimination Settlement," *Athens Daily News*, November 17, 2000, 8A. For an examination of racial discrimination by the Shoney's corporation see Steve Watkins, *The Black O: Racism and Redemption in an American Corporate Empire* (Athens: University of Georgia Press, 1997).

11. For a discussion of these cases see Philip Dine, "Black Workers File Bias Suit against Lockheed Martin; Defense Contractor Has Discriminated in Promotion, Pay and Training, Suit Says," *St. Louis Post-Dispatch*, May 11, 2000, A11; and Edward Iwata, "Race Issues Shake Tech World: What Looks Like Meritocracy Can Brim with Bias, Experts Say as More Lawsuits are Filed," *USA Today* July 24, 2000, 1B.

12. For a discussion of the plight of Black farmers see Armando Villafranca, "Too Little, Too Late; Black Farmers' Discrimination Settlement May Not Ease Years of Pain," *Houston Chronicle*, December 5, 1999, A1.

Notes to Appendix

1. For a discussion of the complex ways in which reality is interpreted see Reuben A. B. May and Mary Pattillo-McCoy, "Do You See What I See?: Examining a Collaborative Ethnography," *Qualitative Inquiry* 6 (March 2000): 65–87. For an interesting discussion on the in-

terpretation of ambiguous interactions see Reuben A. B. May, "'The Sid Cartwright Incident and More': An African American Male's Interpretive Narrative of Interracial Encounters at the University of Chicago," in *Studies in Symbolic Interaction* 24, edited by Norman K. Denzin, (New York: Elsevier Science, 2001), 75–100.

BIBLIOGRAPHY

Altheide, David, and Robert Snow. *Media Worlds in the Postjournalism Era*. New York: Aldine, 1991.

Anderson, Elijah. *A Place on the Corner*. Chicago: University of Chicago Press, 1978.

Anderson, Elijah. *Streetwise: Race, Class, and Change in an Urban Community*. Chicago: University of Chicago Press, 1990.

Anderson, Elijah. *Code of the Street: Decency, Violence, and the Moral Life of the Inner City*. New York: Norton, 1999.

Armstrong, Edward. "The Rhetoric of Violence in Rap and Country Music." *Sociological Inquiry* 63(1) (1993): 64–83.

Bay, Mia. *The White Image in the Black Mind: African-American Ideas about White People, 1830–1925*. New York: Oxford University Press, 2000.

Bell, Michael. *The World from Brown's Lounge: An Ethnography of Black Middle-Class Play*. Urbana: University of Illinois Press, 1983.

Bielby, William, and Denise Bielby. "All Hits Are Flukes: Institutional-
    ized Decision Making and the Rhetoric of Network Prime-Time
    Program Development." *American Journal of Sociology* 99(5)
    (1994): 1287–1313.

Bielby, Denise, and C. Lee Harrington. "Reach Out and Touch Some-
    one: Viewers, Agency, and Audiences in the Televisual Experience."
    In *Viewing, Reading, Listening,* edited by Jon Cruz and Justin Lewis.
    Boulder, Colo.: Westview, 1994, 81–100.

Blumer, Herbert. *Symbolic Interactionism: Perspective and Method.*
    Berkeley: University of California Press, 1987.

Broman, Clifford, Harold Neighbors, and James Jackson, "Racial Group
    Identification among Black Adults." *Social Forces* 67 (1988): 146–
    158.

Brooks, Roy. *Rethinking The American Race Problem.* Berkeley: Uni-
    versity of California Press, 1990.

Cannon, Lou. *Official Negligence: How Rodney King and the Riots
    Changed Los Angeles and the LAPD.* New York: Times Books, 1997.

Carter, Stephen. *Reflections of an Affirmative Action Baby.* New York:
    Basic Books, 1991.

Cavan, Sherri. *Liquor License: An Ethnography of Bar Behavior.* Chi-
    cago: Aldine, 1966.

Chideya, Farai. *Don't Believe the Hype: Fighting Cultural Misinfor-
    mation about African-Americans.* New York: Plume, 1995.

Collins, Sharon M. "Blacks on the Bubble: The Vulnerability of Black
    Executives in White Corporations." *Sociological Quarterly* 34
    (1993): 429–447.

Corcoran, Mary, and Sharon Parrot. "African American Women's Eco-
    nomic Progrss." In *African American and Latina Women at Work:
    Race, Gender, and Economic Inequality.* New York: Russell Sage,
    1998.

Davis, Murray. *What's So Funny? The Comic Conception of Culture
    and Society.* Chicago: University of Chicago Press, 1993.

Drake, St. Clair, and Horace Cayton. *Black Metropolis: A Study of
    Negro Life in a Northern City.* Revised and enlarged. Chicago: Uni-
    versity of Chicago Press, [1945] 1993.

D'Souza, Dinesh. *The End of Racism: Principles of a Multiracial Soci-
    ety.* New York: Free Press, 1995.

Duneier, Mitchell. *Slim's Table: Race, Respectability and Masculinity.*
    Chicago: University of Chicago, 1992.

Farley, Reynolds, and Walter R. Allen. *The Color Line and the Quality of American Life.* New York: Russell Sage Foundation, 1987.

Farmer, Paul. *AIDS and Accusation: Haiti and the Geography of Blame.* Berkeley: University of California Press, 1992.

Feagin, Joe, and Melvin P. Sikes. *Living with Racism: The Black Middle Class Experience.* Boston: Beacon Press, 1994.

Fiske, John. *Television Culture.* London: Methuen, 1987.

Fiske, John. "The Cultural Economy of Fandom." In *The Adoring Audience: Fan Culture and Popular Media,* edited by L. Lewis. New York: Routledge, 1992, 30–49.

Fordham, Signithia, and John Ogbu. "Black Students Success and Coping with the Burden of Acting White." *Urban Review* 18 (1986): 176–206.

Fredrickson, George. *The Black Image in the White Mind: The Debate on Afro-American Character and Destiny, 1817–1914.* New York: Harper and Row, 1977; reprinted, Middletown, Conn.: Wesleyan University Press, 1987.

Gamson, Joshua. *Claims to Fame: Celebrity in Contemporary America.* Berkeley: University of California Press, 1994.

Gillespie, Marie. *Television, Ethnicity, and Cultural Change.* New York: Routledge, 1995.

Goffman, Erving. *Presentations of Self in Everyday Life.* New York: Anchor Books, 1959.

Goffman, Erving. *Interaction Ritual: Essays in Face-to-Face Behavior.* Chicago: Aldine, 1967.

Goldscheider, Frances, and Linda Waite. *New Families, No Families?: The Transformation of the American Home.* Berkeley: University of California Press, 1991.

Graves, Sherryl Browne. "Television and Prejudice Reduction: When Does Television as a Vicarious Experience Make a Difference?" *Journal of Social Issues* 55(4) (Winter 1999): 707–727.

Groh, Dieter. "The Temptation of Conspiracy Theory, or: Why Do Bad Things Happen to Good People?" In *Changing Conceptions of Conspiracy,* edited by Carl F. Graumann and Serge Moscovici. New York: Springer-Verlag, 1987, 1–37.

Grover, Chris, and Keith Soothill. "Ethnicity, The Search for Rapists and the Press." *Ethnic and Racial Studies* (19) (July 1996): 567–584.

Gwaltney, John. *Drylongso: A Self-Portrait of Black America.* New York: Random House, 1980.

Halle, David. *America's Working Man: Work, Home, and Politics among Blue-Collar Property Owners.* Chicago: University of Chicago Press, 1984.

Hannerz, Ulf. *Soul Side: Inquiries into Ghetto Culture and Community.* New York: Columbia University Press, 1969.

Hawkeswood, William. *One of the Children: Gay Black Men in Harlem.* Edited by Alex Costley. Berkeley: University of California Press, 1996.

Hobson, Dorothy. "Housewives and the Mass Media." In *Culture, Media, Language,* edited by Stuart Hall, Dorothy Hobson, Andrew Lowe, and Paul Willis. London: Unwin Hyman, 1980, 105–114.

Hofstadter, Richard. "The Paranoid Style in American Politics." In *The Fear of Conspiracy: Images of Un-American Subversion from the Revolution to the Present,* edited by David B. Davis. Ithaca, N.Y.: Cornell University Press, 1971, 2–8.

Horton, David, and Robert Wohl, "Mass Communication and Parasocial Interaction," *Psychiatry* 19 (1956): 215–224.

Hudson, Shawna. "Recreational Television: The Paradox of Change and Continuity within Stereotypical Iconography." *Sociological Inquiry* 68(2) (1998): 242–257.

Jenkins, Henry. *Textual Poachers: Television Fans and Participatory Culture.* London: Routledge, 1992.

Jensen, John. "Fandom as Pathology: The Consequences of Characterization." In *The Adoring Audience: Fan Culture and Popular Media,* edited by L. Lewis (New York: Routledge, 1992), 9–29.

Jones, James. *Bad Blood: The Tuskegee Syphilis Experiment.* New York: Free Press, 1993.

Katovich, Michael, and William Reese II. "The Regular: Full-time Identities and Membership in an Urban Bar." *Journal of Contemporary Ethnography* 16 (1987): 308–343.

Keiser, R. Lincoln. *The Vice Lords: Warriors of the Streets.* New York: Holt, Rinehart and Winston, 1969.

Knopf, Terry Ann. *Rumors Race and Riots.* New Brunswick, N.J.: Transaction Books, 1975.

Lemann, Nicholas. *The Promised Land: The Great Black Migration and How It Changed America.* New York: Vintage Books, 1991.

LeMasters, E. E. *Blue-Collar Aristocrat: Life-styles at a Working-Class Tavern.* Madison: University of Wisconsin Press, 1975.

Lemish, David. "Soap Opera Viewing in College: A Naturalistic Inquiry," *Journal of Broadcasting and Electronic Media* 29 (1985): 275–292.

Marks, Carol. *Farewell—We're Good and Gone.* Bloomington: Indiana University Press, 1989.

Massey, Douglass, and Nancy Denton. *American Apartheid: Segregation and the Making of the Underclass.* Cambridge, Mass.: Harvard University Press, 1993.

Massey, Douglass, Gretchen A. Condran, and Nancy A. Denton. "The Effect of Residential Segregation on Black Social and Economic Well-Being." *Social Forces* 66 (1987): 29–57.

May, Reuben A. B. "'The Sid Cartwright Incident and More': An African American Male's Interpretive Narrative of Interracial Encounters at the University of Chicago." In *Studies in Symbolic Interaction* 24, edited by Norman K. Denzin, New York: Elsevier Science, 2001, 75–100.

May, Reuben A. B., and Mary Pattillo-McCoy. "Do You See What I See?: Examining a Collaborative Ethnography." *Qualitative Inquiry* 6 (March 2000): 65–87.

Modleski, Tania. *Loving with a Vengeance: Mass-Produced Fantasies for Women.* New York: Routledge, 1982.

Morley, David. *Nationwide Audience.* London: British Film Institute, 1980.

Murphy, Sheila T. "The Impact of Factual versus Fictional Media Portrayals on Cultural Stereotypes." *Annals of the American Academy of Political and Social Science* 560 (November 1998): 165–178.

Murray, Charles, and Richard Herrnstein. *The Bell Curve: Intelligence and Class Structure in American Life.* New York: Simon and Schuster, 1994.

Oldenburg, Ray. *The Great Good Place: Cafés, Coffee Shops, Community Centers, Beauty Parlors, General Stores, Bars, Hangouts, and How They Get You through the Day.* New York: Marlowe, [1989] 1997.

Oliver, Mary Beth. "Caucasian Viewers' Memory of Black and White Criminal Suspects in the News." *Journal of Communication* 49(3) (Summer 1999): 46–60.

Oliver, Melvin L., and Thomas M. Shapiro. *Black Wealth/White Wealth: A New Perspective on Racial Inequality.* New York: Routledge, 1995.

O'Neill, June, and Solomon Polachek. "Why the Gender Gap in Wages Narrowed in the 1980s." *Journal of Labor Economics* 11 (1993): 205–228.

Padilla, Felix. *The Gang as An American Enterprise.* New Brunswick: Rutgers University Press, 1992.

Pattillo-McCoy, Mary. *Black Picket Fences: Privilege and Peril among the Black Middle Class.* Chicago: University of Chicago Press, 1999.

Peffley, Mark, Todd Shields, and Bruce Williams. "The Intersection of Race and Crime in Television News Stories: An Experimental Study." *Political Communication* 13 (July–September 1996): 309–327.

Perse, Elizabeth, and Rebecca Rubin. "Attribution in Social and Parasocial Relationships." *Communication Research* 16 (1989): 59–77.

Pettiway, Leon. *Honey, Honey Miss Thang: Being Black, Gay and on the Streets.* Philadelphia: Temple University Press, 1996.

Rogers, Stacy, and Paul Amato. "Is Marital Quality Declining? The Evidence from Two Generations." *Social Forces* 75(3) (March 1997): 1089–1100.

Root, Judy A. *Changing Families.* Belmont, Calif.: Wadsworth, 1994.

Rose, Tricia. *Black Noise: Rap Music and Black Culture in Contemporary America.* Hanover, N.H.: Wesleyan University Press, 1994.

Sasson, Theodore. "African American Conspiracy Theories and the Social Construction of Crime." *Sociological Inquiry* 65 (3/4) (1995): 265–285.

Schuman, Howard, Charlotte Steeh, and Lawrence Bobo. *Racial Attitudes in America: Trends and Interpretations.* Cambridge, Mass.: Harvard University Press, 1985.

Sigelman, Lee, and Susan Welch. "The Contact Hypothesis Revisited: Black-White Interaction and Positive Racial Attitudes." *Social Forces* 71(3) (1993): 781–795.

Simmel, Georg. *On Individuality and Social Forms.* Reprint. Chi-cago: University of Chicago Press, [1910] 1971.

Smeltzer, Larry R., and Terry Leap. "An Analysis of Individual Reactions to Potentially Offensive Jokes in Work Settings." *Human Relations* 41(4) (April 1988): 295–304.

Smith, Christopher B. "Back and to the Future: The Intergroup Contact Hypothesis Revisited." *Sociological Inquiry* 64(4) (November 1994): 438–455.

Spain, Daphne, and Suzanne M. Bianchi. *Balancing Act: Motherhood, Marriage, and Employment among American Women.* New York: Russell Sage Foundation, 1996.

Spear, Allan H. *Black Chicago: The Making of a Negro Ghetto: 1890–1920.* Chicago: University of Chicago Press, 1967.

Spradley, James, and Brenda Mann. *The Cocktail Waitress: Woman's Work in a Man's World.* New York: Wiley, 1975.

Suttles, Gerald. *The Social Order of the Slum: Ethnicity and Territory in the Inner City.* Chicago: University of Chicago Press, 1968.

Swidler, Ann. "Culture in Action: Symbols and Strategies." *American Sociological Review* 51 (1986): 273–286.

Turner, Patricia. *I Heard It through the Grapevine: Rumor in African American Culture.* Berkeley: University of California Press, 1993.

Waite, Linda. "Does Marriage Matter?" *Demography* 32(4) (November 1995): 483–507.

Waters, Anita. "Conspiracy Theories as Ethnosociologies: Explanation and Intention in African American Political Culture." *Journal of Black Studies* 28(1) (1997): 112–125.

Watkins, Steve. *The Black O: Racism and Redemption in an American Corporate Empire.* Athens: University of Georgia Press, 1997.

Wellington, Alison J. "The Male/Female Wage Gap among Whites: 1976 and 1985." *American Sociological Review* 59 (1994): 839–848.

Wilson, William J. *The Declining Significance of Race: Blacks and Changing American Institutions.* 2nd ed. Chicago: University of Chicago Press, 1980.

Wilson, William J. *The Truly Disadvantaged: The Inner City, the Underclass and Public Policy.* Chicago: University of Chicago Press, 1987.

Wilson, William J. *When Work Disappears: The World of the New Urban Poor.* New York: Knopf, 1996.

Wilson, William J. *Over the Racial Divide: Rising Inequality and Coalition Politics.* Berkeley: University of California Press, 1999.

Wulff, Erich. "Paranoic Conspiratory Delusion." In *Changing Conceptions of Conspiracy,* edited by Carl F. Graumann and Serge Moscovici. New York: Springer-Verlag, 1987, 177–190.

INDEX

ABOUT THE AUTHOR

Reuben A. Buford May was born in Chicago on April 3, 1965, and is the eldest of three sons. He attended elementary and secondary schools in Chicago. After graduation from Kenwood Academy High School, he attended Aurora University, where in 1987 he received a B.A. in criminal justice. In 1991, he received a Master of Art Degree in sociology from DePaul University. After working in the social work field for two years, he entered the University of Chicago to pursue a Ph.D. in sociology. In 1996, he received his Ph.D. from the university.

Professor May is currently an assistant professor of sociology in the department of sociology at the University of Georgia. He has been nominated for and won university-wide undergraduate teaching awards, and he has published scholarly articles in the areas of race, collective memory, qualitative methods, and the

sociology of sport. In addition to his scholarly interests he is also
a mentor for Athens-area youth and a volunteer varsity assistant coach for boys basketball at one of the area high schools. He
lives in Athens, Georgia, with his wife, Lyndel, and daughters,
Tamarra and Regina.